Dart Programming For Complete Beginners

Irene .U Shaffer

Introduction

This book serves as an introductory guide to the Dart programming language, providing readers with essential knowledge and practical guidance for starting their journey in Dart development.

The guide begins by establishing the scope of the content and proceeds to walk readers through the process of setting up the Dart SDK and Visual Studio Code. It emphasizes using various development environments, including text editors, command prompts, terminals, shells, and DartPad.

The syntax section introduces fundamental concepts like statements, comments, blocks, identifiers, and keywords. The guide then dives into basic program components, offering a hands-on example with a "Hello World!" Dart application.

Data types are explored in detail, covering numbers, strings, booleans, lists, and maps. The explanation of variables includes dynamic typing and string interpolation, providing a solid foundation for readers to understand and use these concepts effectively.

User input is addressed, guiding readers on how to read numbers and make decisions using if-else and switch-case constructs. The guide further covers loops, functions, and explores working with lists and maps in Dart.

In-depth coverage of maps includes discussions on HashMap, LinkedHashMap, iteration using forEach, and various methods to manipulate and interact with map data. The guide also touches on more advanced topics, such as using maps in loops and dealing with lists of maps.

The final section introduces object-oriented programming (OOP) in Dart, providing a foundational understanding of this paradigm and setting the stage for readers to advance their Dart programming skills.

In summary, this book offers a comprehensive and accessible introduction to Dart, making it an ideal resource for those starting their programming journey or looking to add Dart to their skill set. The guide's hands-on approach, clear explanations, and practical examples contribute to a valuable learning experience for beginners in Dart development.

Contents

1. Overview

Dart is a multi-paradigm programming language developed by Google. It supports the following programming paradigms – object oriented programming (OOP), functional, imperative and reflective. In October 2012, Dart was unveiled at the GOTO conference in Denmark. Computer Scientist Lars Bak and Software Engineer Kasper Lund are the founding members of Dart programming language.

The first version of Dart (Dart 1.0) was released on November 14, 2013 and at the time of writing this book (December 2021), the latest stable version is Dart 2.15.1. Syntactically, this language is similar to Java and JavaScript. In fact, people who are familiar with both Java and JavaScript will say that Dart looks like a combination of Java and JavaScript.

The development tools needed for Dart are made available for Windows, Linux and macOS using BSD licence. These tools can build applications for the web, desktop, etc.

2. Scope

Using Dart, you can build applications for the web, desktop applications, server side applications, mobile applications, etc. There is a mobile application development framework called **Flutter** developed by Google which is entirely written in Dart and it uses Dart to write code and thus build mobile apps. Technically speaking, web applications built using Dart can run inside web browsers. This is made possible by the Dart to JavaScript compiler (**dart2js**) included inside the Dart SDK.

What will I learn from this Book?

This book will teach you to build console based Dart applications for Desktops. You will start by installing and configuring Dart on your system, learn how to compile and execute code. Further, you will begin learning the actual programming concepts and start building your own Dart apps. There is not much difference between a desktop app and a server side app. This means, the concepts that you will learn to build desktop apps will also be useful in building server side apps.

Will I learn web development or mobile app development?

Mobile application development through Dart is done using the Flutter framework which is a different story altogether. In order to learn web application development using any framework, basic knowledge of HTML, CSS and JavaScript is needed. Hence, covering mobile application development and web application development is beyond the scope of this book. However, the basic concepts of Dart programming language will be covered which will server as a stepping stone for learning advanced concepts.

What are the prerequisites of learning Dart?

No prior programming experience is needed to learn Dart. Having said that, previous programming experience in C/C++, Java or JavaScript will definitely help. Again, if you have not written a single program in your whole life, Dart could be the first! This book has been written keeping the absolute beginner in mind. So, follow along, do not skip chapters and you should be able to pick up concepts with ease. However, you should be comfortable with your system/OS. You should be well-versed with moving files around, working with archives, installing/uninstalling software and most importantly – being comfortable with Command Prompt or PowerShell or Terminal/Shell.

3. Environment Setup

Dart SDK is is needed in order to run Dart code on your system. There are different ways of doing this depending on the operating system in use. We will follow a method which is more or less the same for Windows, Linux and macOS.

3.1 Setup Dart SDK

We will be setting up the Dart SDK on Windows and on a Unix-like OS. All of the programs demonstrated in this book have been written and tested on Windows. These programs should work fine on other operating systems as long as there is no operating system specific code.

Visit https://dart.dev/get-dart/archive and download the latest version of the Dart SDK for your OS. Once you have the archive, extract it to a convenient location. Now, go to the location where this archive has been extracted, locate the *bin* folder inside the *dart-sdk* folder.

3.1.1 Dart SDK on Windows

Once you have located the bin directory (for example C:\dart-sdk\bin), add path to this bin directory to the *Path* environment variable. On Windows, you can launch *System Properties -> Advanced system properties -> Environment Variables* and add path to the bin directory to the existing contents of this variable. Be sure to add a semicolon at the end of the previous contents of the Path variable if it is not present. Here is what the variable contents should look like:

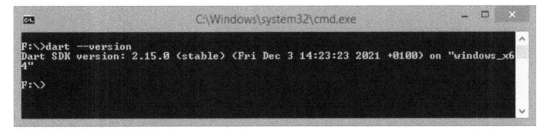

To check if the installation is successful, open Command Prompt/Powershell on Windows and enter the following command:

dart --version

If you see something like this, it means that the setup is successful:

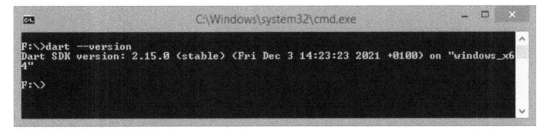

If you see an error which says something like command not found, it can either mean that the Path variable has not been correctly set or there is a problem with the SDK itself. In such cases, follow the whole setup process from the beginning right from downloading the appropriate SDK version for your OS.

3.1.2 Dart SDK on Unix-like OS (Linux, macOS, FreeBSD, etc.)

On Linux, macOS, FreeBSD, etc., open *~/.bashrc* or *~/.bash_profile* and add the following line at the bottom:

> *export PATH=$PATH:(path to the bin directory without brackets)*
> *Example:*
> *export PATH=$PATH:/home/user/dart-sdk/bin*

This statement will add the path to the **bin** directory to the **PATH** environment variable. We do this to enable us to access the SDK from anywhere and not just from the working directory. Here is what the file should look like:

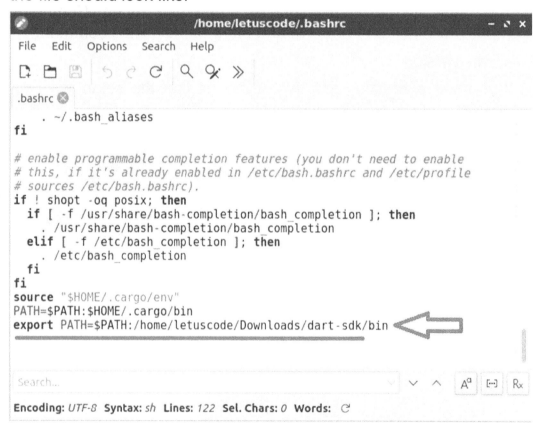

Save this file and close the editor. Open Terminal/Shell and enter the following command:

echo $PATH

This command will show the contents of the PATH variable. If you carried out the previous step properly, you should see the path of dart-sdk's bin directory added to this variable:

Now, enter the following command:

dart --version

You should see the following:

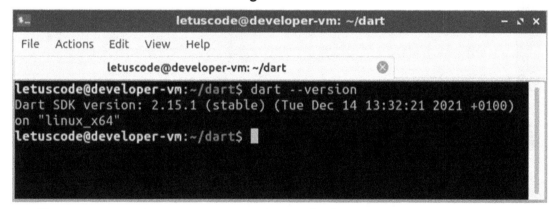

If you encounter an error, go through the set up process again.

For more information on other methods of installing Dart, visit https://dart.dev/get-dart.

3.2 Set up Visual Studio Code

Dart programs can be written in any code editor or text editor. In this section, we will demonstrate how to set up Visual Studio Code (VS Code) to build Dart applications. This part is optional, you may completely avoid this section and write Dart programs using your favourite text editor such as Notepad++, Wordpad, Notepad, Atom, etc. The reason behind choosing Visual Studio Code is that there is something for everyone in this code editor. Right from beginners to advanced programmers, everyone will find a feature that they will find useful.

Visit https://code.visualstudio.com/ and download the stable installation file for your OS. Execute the installation file and follow the instructions. The installation process is straight forward and should not need any special instructions. Make sure that you have administrator rights before going ahead with the installation.

Run the Visual Studio Code application once the installation is over. You will see a window like this:

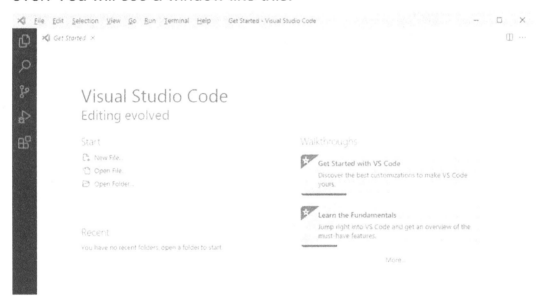

This code editor does not include support for Dart by default. So, we will have to install an extension. Click on **Extensions** or **Manage -> Extensions** or simply press **Ctrl + Shift + X.** Search for Dart and click install once the extension has been found:

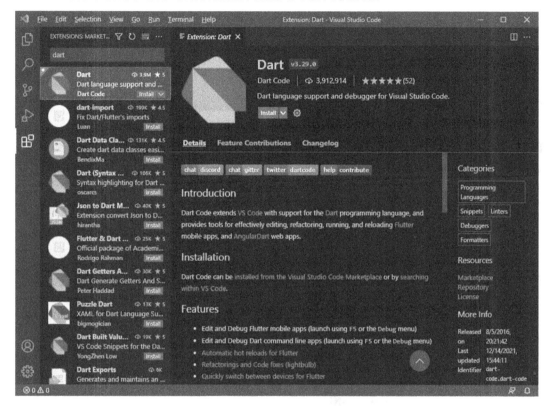

The installation will take a few minutes to complete. Once done, restart VS Code. If you would like to use some other editor or an IDE, visit https://dart.dev/tools to learn more.

Note: In the next chapter, you will learn to run Dart code through VS Code and also through the Command Prompt/ Shell /Terminal.

4. Compile and Execute Dart Code

There are different ways to run Dart code. The SDK can build applications targeted for Web, Desktop/Server and Mobile Devices (via Flutter). For building web applications, there is a source-to-source Dart to JavaScript compiler called ***dart2js***. Since major web browsers support JavaScript by default, there is no need for them to add support for Dart. We will not be developing web applications or mobile applications. We will only be building console applications that run on PC. These applications can also be looked at as server side applications. Most of the applications demonstrated in this book will not have enterprise grade significance and are built only to explain basic Dart programming concepts. As you continue to learn Dart fundamentals, you may try to build Dart applications which have real life significance.

For building Dart applications that run on PC/Server, there are two types of compilation methods – ***Just-in-time compilation (JIT)*** and ***Ahead-of-time compilation (AOT)***. The Dart SDK ships with a cross platform Dart Virtual Machine (Dart VM). When using JIT compilation, the Dart code is executed inside the Dart VM. The Dart code is compiled just before execution; hence the name – just in time. Where as, when using AOT compilation, the Dart code is first compiled to platform specific native code. This native code is a self contained stand alone executable file (For eg - .exe file on Windows). The executable file can then be run only on the platform it is built for. AOT method generates executable ahead of time, hence the name. We will learn to use both these compilation methods but most of the Dart programs demonstrated in the book use the JIT method. There are advantages and disadvantages of both these approaches, you may use either one as the context requires. For example, the executable code generated using AOT method will run only on the platform it is built for. But since it is native code, execution will be the fastest and is suited for performance critical applications. On the other hand, applications built using JIT will run on any platform (as long as there is no platform specific code). But since the applications will run inside a VM, the execution will be slightly slower (you will hardly notice any difference on modern computer hardware). JIT is not preferred when performance is the priority.

Let us now go ahead and learn how to compile and execute Dart programs.

4.1 Using Text editor and Command Prompt/Terminal/Shell

Dart programs are simple plaintext files carrying the *.dart* extension. Open your favourite text editor, copy-paste the following code and save it as *firstprogram.dart* at a convenient location:

```
void main() {
print("First Dart program executed successfully!!!");

}
```

This is a Dart program, also known as source file, source code, program or source. We will now learn how to execute this code on different operating systems using different compilation techniques.

Note: You do not have to understand at this stage what this program does and how to write one, we are only learning how to run Dart code. Chapters following this one are filled with programming concepts which will teach you to write your own programs from scratch.

4.1.1 Just-In-Time Compilation (JIT)

The JIT compilation procedure remains the same across all operating systems. Open Command Prompt/Powershell/ Terminal /Shell, navigate to the directory where *firstprogram.dart* has been saved. Let us now see how to use different compilation methods:

To execute Dart program using JIT, enter the following command:

dart run <dart program name>

For the program that we just wrote, substitute **<dart program name>** with **firstprogram.dart**:

dart run firstprogram.dart

Here is what you should see inside Command Prompt/ Powershell on Windows:

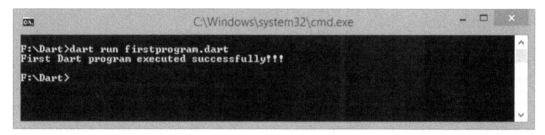

Here is what you should see inside Terminal/Shell on Unix-like OS (Linux, macOS, etc):

4.1.2 Ahead-Of-Time Compilation (AOT)

Ahead of time compilation generates platform specific native executable file. Here is how to compile Dart code using AOT:

4.1.2.1 Dart AOT compilation on Windows

Open Command Prompt/Powershell, navigate to the directory where **firstprogram.dart** has been saved and enter the following command to AOT compile a Dart program into an executable file:

dart compile exe <dart program name>

For the program that we just wrote, substitute **<dart program name>** with **firstprogram.dart**:

dart compile exe firstprogram.dart

The above command will build an executable file having the same name as that of the program with the extension .exe. For example, after successfully compiling firstprogram.dart, firstprogram.exe will be generated. Here is what you should see after successful compilation:

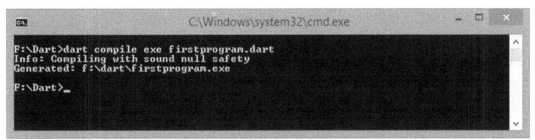

The executable can then be run inside the Command Prompt /Powershell as follows:

<generated file name>.exe
Example:
firstprogram.exe

Here is what you should see after executing firstprogram.exe:

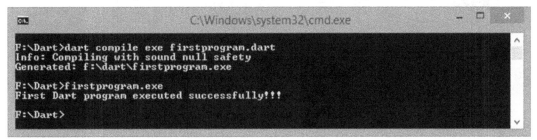

4.1.2.2 Dart AOT compilation on Unix-like OS (Linux, macOS, FreeBSD, etc.)

On Unix-like operating systems, open Terminal/Shell, navigate to the directory where **firstprogram.dart** has been saved and enter the following command to AOT compile a Dart program into an executable binary:

dart compile exe <dart program name> -o <output file name>

For the program that we just wrote, substitute **<dart program name>** with **firstprogram.dart** and **<output file name>** could be anything but it is ideal to keep the output file name same as the source file name without the extension:

dart compile exe firstprogram.dart -o firtstprogram

The above command will build an executable file having the same name as specified in the **<output file name>** filed. In this case, it will be **firstprogram**. You should see the following once AOT compilation is successful:

You may run **ls -l** command to determine whether the executable file has been generated with the right permissions:

As seen, **firstprogram** file has **execute** permission. You may run it as:

./<output file name>
Example:
./firstprogram

You should see the following once firstprogram has been executed successfully:

4.2 Using Visual Studio Code

Open Visual Studio Code, click **File -> New**. A new empty file will open in a new tab. Copy-paste the following code inside the empty file:

```
void main() {
print("First Dart program executed successfully!!!");
}
```

Click **File -> Save** or press **Ctrl + S**. Give the file a name, select the file type as **Dart** and save it at a convenient location. Here is what the editor window should look like:

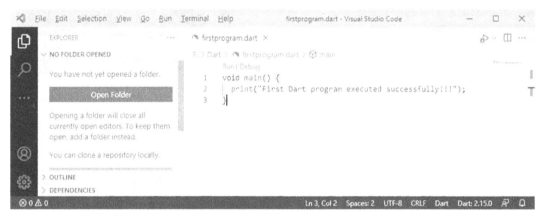

Click **Run -> Run Without Debugging** or press **Ctrl + F5**.

The program should run in the Debug Console as follows:

If the Debug Console is not visible after running the code, click **View -> Debug Console**.

Note: It does not matter which OS or editor you use. It is best to stick to the tools you are the most comfortable with. As far as compilation methods are concerned, which one to use will depend on the situation and the desired end goal. We will use JIT compilation for most of the programs.

4.3 DartPad

DartPad is an online tool meant for trying out Dart. This tool can be accessed using any modern Web browser such as Firefox, Google Chrome, Opera, Brave, etc. To use DartPad, visit https://dartpad.dev/. The editor on the left side is where you will write your Dart programs. The console on the right side will display the output of your program.

Copy-paste the sample Dart program from the previous section inside the DartPad editor and click Run button. You should see the following output:

Note: DartPad is a good tool for testing purpose. You cannot build proper applications using this tool. While learning Dart programming, using DartPad is a good choice along with other options explained in previous sections.

5. Syntax

Before moving ahead, make sure that you are really comfortable with the OS/tools you will be writing your Dart programs on because from now on you will be learning the actual programming concepts to be able to build stand-alone Dart applications. Hence, it is important that you are comfortable with compiling and executing Dart code.

Dart is a case-sensitive programming language. We may treat the same words in different cases as the same but Dart language will treat them differently. For example, words "Dart Programming", "DART programming" and "dart PROGRAMMING" may look the same to us but each word will be treated differently by the compiler.

5.1 Statements

A statement is a line of code that carries out a meaningful computational task. These tasks can be anything such as adding numbers, printing something on the console, reading from the user, writing to a file, etc. Statements in Dart end with a semi-colon (;). You can have as many statements as you want on a single line but it is a good programming practice to have one statement on one line. This promotes code readability. Some examples of statements are:

```
print("Hi from Dart");
int x = 30;
int y = 66;
var product = x * y;
```

5.2 Comments

Comments are ignored by the compiler and hence have no outcome on the output of the program. There are no rules as such regarding the usage of comments. Developers use comments to mark or explain a piece of code; can also carry notes for other developers. Dart offers single-line and block comments (multi-line comments). Single line comments begin with **double-slash (//)** and must terminate on the same line. Block comments can span across multiple lines are enclosed within this character sequence – **slash-asterisk (/*)** and asterisk-slash **(*/).**

Single line comments:

//This is a comment
//This is another single-line

Block comments:

/*
This is line one
This is line two
This is line 3
*/

Note: There are many programming examples in this book. Each program has comments in it to explain the working of the code. While learning the program, be sure to read the comments to better understand the program.

5.3 Blocks

A block of code in Dart is a group of statements enclosed within curly brackets ({ }). Here is an example:

{
print("Hello");
print("This is a Dart programming block!");
}

Blocks are used heavily in decision making, loops, functions, etc.

5.4 Identifiers

Identifiers are used to identify classes, objects, variables, functions, etc. Identifier names can contain alphanumeric characters, dollar sign ($) and underscore (_); but has to start with either an underscore or an alphabet.

5.5 Keywords

Keywords in any programming language are reserved words which cannot be used as identifier names. Keywords have a specific meaning which tells the end application what to do. To know more about the available keywords in Dart, visit: https://dart.dev/guides/language/language-tour#keywords.

5.6 Basic program components

Writing a basic stand-alone Dart program is very simple. All you need to do is write a *main function* which serves as an entry point to the program. That is, the program will begin executing from the first statement inside the main function till the last one. Here is the general syntax to write the main function:

```
void main() {
//Statement 1
//Statement 2
...
...
...
//Statement n
}
```

6. Hello World! Dart Application

In this chapter, we will learn to write our first meaningful Dart program that prints *Hello World!* On the console. We have learnt in the previous section that the basic requirement of a stand-alone Dart program is a main function. This function will serve as an entry point. Inside this function, we will place a statement that prints some text on the console (Hello World! in this case). We will use the ***print*** function to print text on the screen. The simplest form of text can be looked at as a string in programmatic terms. A string is a sequence of characters. Here is a general syntax of using the print function:

print("<string>");
Example:
print("Hi!");

Let us now put together whatever we have learnt and build an application that prints Hello World! On the console. Here is the program:

```dart
//Mandatory main function of a Dart program
void main() {
    //Program execution will begin from here
    //print function to print Hello World! on the console
    print("Hello World!");
}
```

Output:

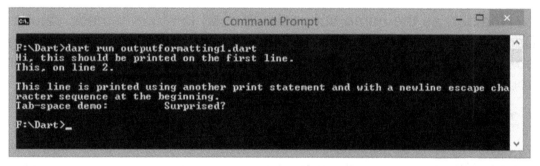

```
F:\Dart>dart run HelloWorld.dart
Hello World!

F:\Dart>
```

You can make use of escape character sequences such as **\n** for new line and **\t** for tab-space. Here is a demo:

```
//Mandatory main function of a Dart program
void main() {
    //Program execution will begin from here
    //print function to print something on the console
    print("Hi, this should be printed on the first line.\nThis, on line 2.");
    print("\nThis line is printed using another print statement and with a newline escape
character sequence at the beginning.");
    print("Tab-space demo:\t\tSurprised?");
}
```

Output:

```
F:\Dart>dart run outputformatting1.dart
Hi, this should be printed on the first line.
This, on line 2.

This line is printed using another print statement and with a newline escape cha
racter sequence at the beginning.
Tab-space demo:         Surprised?

F:\Dart>_
```

Note: If you want to print restricted characters (such as double-quotes) inside a string, you can escape it using a backslash. Example:

print("\nThis is a double quote ==> \" ");

23

7. Data Types

A data type is used to categorize data. For example, if we want to store the name of a person, we will do it in a string form whereas, age will be stored in numeric form. These two parameters belong to two different data types. Dart is a *type safe* language. That it, it uses static and runtime type checking to make sure that the data of a variable matches its static type. This is also known as *sound typing*. Since Dart is type safe, every piece of data that is present in the application will have a data type. However, type annotation (specifying the data type) is optional. This is because of a feature called as *type inference* where in the data type is assumed based on the data stored. For example, if name of a person is stored in a variable, the data type will be inferred as string.

Dart supports the following data types – Number, String, Boolean, List and Map.

7.1 Number

Number, as the name suggests, is used to store numeric values. Dart supports two types of numbers – *integer* and *double (floating point values)*. The data type for integers is *int* where as that for double is *double*.

7.2 String

A string is a sequence of characters. The data type for string is *String*. When a constant string is used, the sequence of characters is enclosed within double-quotes. For example, in the previous chapter where we learned to print Hello World! on the console, we used the constant string "Hello World!" and passed it to the *print* function.

7.3 Boolean

A boolean data type can be either *true* or *false*. In digital electronics or boolean algebra terms, true or false can be referred to as 0 (false) or 1 (true) / low (false) or high (true). The data type used for Boolean is *bool*.

7.4 List

A list is a collection, an ordered group of objects. It is similar to arrays in programming languages like C/C++, Java, C#, etc. The data type used for list is *List*.

7.5 Map

A map is a data structure which stores data in key-value pairs. For every unique key, there will be corresponding value. The data type used here is *Map*.

8. Variables

A variable is a name given to a memory location. When we store data, it resides in the memory where a memory region is reserved for it based on its type. This region can be uniquely addressed using its memory address which is usually represented in hexadecimal form. Since it would be difficult to memorize addresses, we have variables. Here is a general syntax of declaring variables in Dart:

<data type> <variable name>;
Example:
int num;
double temp;
String name;
bool flag;

It is possible to initialize variables by assigning some values to them at the time of declaration using the following syntax:

<data type> <variable name> = <initial value>;
Example:
int num = -500;
double temp = 15.7;
String name = "Rey";
bool flag = true;

Multiple variables of the same type can be declared in one statement by separating them using commas as follows:

<data type> <variable1 name>, <variable2 name>, ... , <variable2 name>;
Example:
int num1, num2, num3;
double x, y, z;
String fname, lname, country;

The value of a variable can be changed at a later point in the program using the **assignment operator** given by the equal to sign (=). The value of a variable can be printed on the console using the print function as follows:

print(<variable>)
Example:
print (num);
print (country);

Let us write a Dart program to declare different variables and print their values:

```dart
//Variables demo -- declare different types of variables and print them
//Mandatory main function of a Dart program
void main() {
//Declare an integer variable and assign some value
int num1 = 45;
//Declare a double value
double num2;
//Assign some value to num2
num2 = 56.12;
//print num1 and num2
print("\nnum1: ");
print(num1);
print("\nnum2: ");
print(num2);
//Declare some string variables and assign values
String str1 = "Some", str2 = "Words";
//Print str1 and str2
print("\nstr1: ");
print(str1);
print("\nstr2: ");
print(str2);
//Declare some boolean variables
bool b1, b2;
//Assign values to b1 and b2
b1 = true;
b2 = false;
print("\nb1: ");
print(b1);
print("\nb2: ");
```

```
print(b2);
}
```
Output:

```
Command Prompt                                          –  □  ×

F:\Dart>dart run variables1.dart

num1:
45

num2:
56.12

str1:
Some

str2:
Words

b1:
true

b2:
false

F:\Dart>
```

8.2 Dynamic type

If you do not want to specify the data type of a variable, dynamic type can be used. Non statically typed variables can be declared using **var** or **dynamic** keyword as follows:

var <variable name>;
dynamic <variable name>;
Example:
var a;
dynamic b;
a = 67;
b = "Hi";

With the type inference feature of Dart, the data type of a non statically typed variable will be determined according to the assigned

28

value. Here is a program that demonstrates the usage of dynamic variables:

```dart
//Variables demo -- dynamic type variables / type inference
//Mandatory main function of a Dart program
void main() {
//Declare dynamic variables using var keyword
var x , y, z;
//Declare dynamic variables using dynamic keyword
dynamic a , b, c;
//Assign values to variables
x = "Zoo";
y = true;
z = 23.124;
a = 45;
b = false;
c = "Greatness!";
//Print everything
print("\nx: ");
print(x);
print("\ny: ");
print(y);
print("\nz: ");
print(z);
print("\na: ");
print(a);
print("\nb: ");
print(b);
print("\nc: ");
print(c);
//Assign values of different type
x = 34;
y = "Hello!";
z = false;
a = -64.65;
b = y;
c = 99;
//Print everything
print("\nx: ");
print(x);
print("\ny: ");
print(y);
print("\nz: ");
print(z);
```

```
print("\na: ");
print(a);
print("\nb: ");
print(b);
print("\nc: ");
print(c);
}
```

Output:

As seen from the above output, non statically typed variables can hold data of different types through the course of the program.

Note:

- The key difference between **dynamic** and **var** keyword is – if a variable is initialized using the var keyword, the data type of that variable cannot change through the course of the program. The value of the variable can change as long as it is of the same data type. Whereas, there are no such restrictions on a variable declared using the dynamic keyword.

- If you want the value of a variable to remain constant throughout the program, you can use the **final** keyword.

8.3 String interpolation

String interpolation is a process of building a string using other variables. This is particularly useful when printing the contents of variables in a systematic manner. Let us understand this concept with the help of an example. Consider the following code snippet:

Say we want to build a meaningful string with these two variables. Something like – "Dear Elgar James, your account number is 325426". Using string interpolation, we can use variables to substitute their values inside a string. The interpolated string will look like:

As see, you can use $<variable name> OR ${ <variable name / expression> } to substitute the value of a variable or the resultant value after evaluating an expression inside a string. You can even use the same syntax to print the value of a variable using print function in a more convenient way. For example:

```
var name = "Elgar James";
int account_num = 325426;
"Dear ${ name }, your account number is ${ account_num }"
print("\nName: $ name \nAge: ${age} ");
```

Let us write a program that demonstrates string interpolation:

```
//Variables demo -- string interpolation
//Mandatory main function of a Dart program
```

```dart
void main() {
//Declare some variables and assign values
String first_name = "Laura";
String last_name = "Larson";

int age = 28;
String country = "USA";
//Print everything with string interpolation
print("\nFirst name: ${ first_name }");
print("\nLast name: ${ last_name }");
print("\nAge: ${ age }");
print("\nCountry: ${ country } \n");
String paragraph = "The name of the person is ${ first_name } ${ last_name }. She is ${ age } years of age and a resident of ${ country }.";
print(paragraph);
}
```

Output:

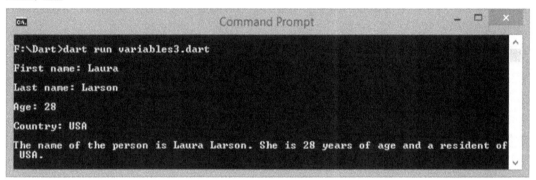

Note: When a variable is declared but not value is assigned to it, in such a case, the variable will have **Null** value.

9. Operators

An operator is a symbol or a set of symbols which carries out a computational task such as adding numbers, comparing variables, checking for a type of a variable, etc. Dart offers the following types of operators – arithmetic operators, comparison operators, type test operators, logical operators, bitwise operators and assignment operators. Let us take a look at each one of these categories.

9.1 Arithmetic operators

Arithmetic operators are used to carry out mathematical operations such as addition, subtraction, multiplication, division, etc.

Operator	Description	Sample Usage	Explanation
+	Addition	x + y	Adds all operands and returns sum.
-	Subtraction	x - y	Subtracts operand on the right from the operand on the left and returns the difference.
*	Multiplication	x * y	Multiplies operands and returns the product.
/	Division	x / y	Performs division and returns the quotient.
~/	Integer Division	x ~/ y	Performs division and returns the quotient in integer form. For example, 5~/ 2 will return 2 and not 2.5.
%	Modulus (Remainder)	x % y	Performs division and returns the remainder. Operands needs to be of integer type.
++	Increment	x++ ++y	Increments the value of the operand by 1. If pre-increment is used (++x), the value will be incremented first and then used. Whereas, in post-increment (x++), the value will be used first and then incremented.
--	Decrement	x-- --y	Decrements the value of the operand by 1. If pre-decrement is used (--x), the value will be decremented first and then used. Whereas, in post-decrement (x--),

Here is a program that demonstrates the use of arithmetic operators:

```dart
//Arithmetic operators demo
//Mandatory main function of a Dart program
void main() {
//Declare some numbers and assign values to them
int num1 = 35, num2 = 13;
//Declare some variables to store the result of arithmetic operations
int sum, difference, product, quotient_int, modulus;
double quotient;
//Perform arithmetic operations
sum = num1 + num2;
difference = num1 - num2;
product = num1 * num2;
quotient = num1 / num2;
quotient_int = num1 ~/ num2;
modulus = num1 % num2;
//Print everything
print("\nnum1 = ${num1} \tnum2 = ${num2}");
print("\nnum1 + num2 = ${sum}");
print("\nnum1 - num2 = ${difference}");

print("\nnum1 * num2 = ${product}");
print("\nnum1 / num2 (Division) = ${quotient}");
print("\nnum1 ~/ num2 (Integer Division) = ${quotient_int}");
print("\nnum1 % num2 = ${modulus}");
//Post-Increment num1 and post-decrement num2
num1++;
num2--;
//Print num1 and num2
print("\nAfter incrementing (post) num1 and num2:\nnum1 = $num1 \tnum2 = ${num2}");
//Pre-Increment num1 and pre-decrement num2 inside print statement
print("\nAfter incrementing (pre) num1 and num2:\nnum1 = ${++num1} \tnum2 = ${--num2}");
}
```

Output:

Multiple operations and terms can be combined to form a mathematical expression. For example, if you want to form this expression ==> $3x^2 + 2$, you can write it as **3 * x * x + 2**. You can even use brackets to make sure that proper order is followed during evaluation ==> **(3 * x * x) + 2**.

Let us write a program to find the value of **f(x)** for **-2 <= x <= 2** where

$f(x) = 3x^2 - 5x + 7$:

```
//Forming expression using arithmetic operators
//Mandatory main function
void main() {
//Declare variable x;
int x;
//Declare some variables to store result
int result;
//Expression f(x) = 3x^2 - 5x + 7
print("\nFunction Expression ---> f(x) = 3x^2 - 5x + 7\n");
//For x = -2
//Set x to -2
x = -2;
//Calculate f(-2)
result = 3 * x * x - 5 * x + 7;
print("For x = $x\tf($x) = $result");
x = -1;
//Calculate f(-1)
```

```
result = 3 * x * x - 5 * x + 7;
print("For x = $x\tf($x) = $result");
x = 0;
//Calculate f(0)
result = (3 * x * x) - (5 * x) + 7;
print("For x = $x\tf($x) = $result");
x = 1;
//Calculate f(1)
result = 3 * x * x - 5 * x + 7;
print("For x = $x\tf($x) = $result");
x = 2;
//Calculate f(2)
result = 3 * x * x - 5 * x + 7;
print("For x = $x\tf($x) = $result");
}
```

Output:

9.2 Comparison operators

Comparison operators are used to compare operands. For example, to check whether a given variable is less than the other, whether two variables are equal, and so on. The result of these operations is either **true** or **false**. Comparison operators are also known as relational operators.

Operator	Description	Sample Usage	Explanation
==	Equal To	x == y	Returns **true** if the values of the given operands are **equal**, **false** otherwise.
!=	Not Equal To	x != y	Returns **true** if the values of the given operands are **NOT equal**, **false** otherwise.

36

<	Less Than	x < y	Returns **true** if the value of the left operand is less than the value of the operand on the right, returns **false** otherwise.
>	Greater Than	x > y	Returns **true** if the value of the left operand is greater than the value of the operand on the right, returns **false** otherwise.
<=	Less Than OR Equal To	x <= y	Returns true if the value of the left operand is less than **OR equal to** the value of the operand on the right, **false** otherwise.
>=	Greater Than OR Equal To	x >= y	Returns **true** if the value of the left operand is greater than **OR equal to** the value of the operand on the right, **false** otherwise.

Here is a program that makes use of comparison operators:

```
//Comparison/Relational operators demo
//Mandatory main function of a Dart program
void main() {
//Declare some variables and assign values to them
int a = 5, b = -3, c = 11, d = -3, x = 19, y = 40;
//Print everything
print("\na = $a, b = $b, c = $c, d = $d, x = $x, y = $y");
//Print results of comparison operations
print("\na > b: ${a > b}");
print("\nc < d: ${c < d}");
print("\nx >= y: ${x >= y}");
print("\ny <= a: ${y <= a}");
print("\nb == d: ${b == d}");
print("\nd != b: ${d != b}");
}
```

Output:

```
F:\Dart>dart run comaprisonoperators.dart
a = 5, b = -3, c = 11, d = -3, x = 19, y = 40
a > b: true
c < d: false
x >= y: false
y <= a: false
b == d: true
d != b: false
F:\Dart>
```

9.3 Type test operators

Type test operators are used to check the data type of a value/variable. Dart offers two type test operators – *is* and *is !* (is not). General syntax:

<value/variable> is <data type>
<value/variable> is !<data type>
Example:
var x = 38, y = -43.12, z = "OOP";
print (x is int);
print (y is double);
print (z is !String);

The *is* operator will return true if the value or the variable is of the given type. For example, from the above code snippet, *x is int* will return true. Whereas, the *is !* Operator will return true if the value/variable is not of the given type. Here is a demonstration of type test operators:

```
//Type Test operators demo
//Mandatory main function of a Dart program
void main() {
//Declare some variables without static typing
var a, b, c;
dynamic x, y, z;
//Assign arbitrary values to these variables
a = 56.87;
b = "UAE";
```

38

```
c = true;
x = 725;
y = false;
z = "Seychelles";
//Print values of all variables
print("\na = $a, b = $b, c = $c\nx = $x, y= $y, z = $z\n");
//Print the results of type testing
print("a is !String: ${a is !String}");
print("a is double: ${a is double}");
print("b is String: ${b is String}");
print("b is bool: ${b is bool}");
print("c is int: ${c is int}");
print("c is !bool: ${c is !bool}");
print("x is int: ${x is int}");
print("x is !int:  ${x is !int}");
print("y is double: ${y is double}");
print("y is !String: ${y is !String}");
print("z is int: ${z is int}");
print("z is String: ${z is String}");
}
```

Output:

```
F:\Dart>dart run typetest.dart

a = 56.87, b = UAE, c = true
x = 725, y= false, z = Seychelles

a is !String: true
a is double: true
b is String: true
b is bool: false
c is int: false
c is !bool: false
x is int: true
x is !int: false
y is double: false
y is !String: true
z is int: false
z is String: true

F:\Dart>
```

9.4 Logical operators

Logical operators are used to carry out logical operations – OR, AND and NOT.

Operator	Description	Sample Usage	Explanation
&&	Logical AND	(Expression 1) && (Expression 2)	Returns *true* if all the operands/expressions are

			true. Returns *false* if any one of the operands/expressions is *false*.
||	Logical OR	(Expression 1) && (Expression 2)	Returns *true* if any of the operands/expressions is *true*. Returns *false* if all of the operands/expressions are *false*.
!	Logical NOT	!(Expression 1)	Inverts the value of the given operand. If the expression/operand is *true*, *false* will be returned and if the expression/operand is *false*, *true* will be returned.

Let us write a Dart program to carry out logical operations:

```
//Logical operators demo
//Mandatory main function of a Dart program
void main() {
//Declare some variables
int x = 23, y = 66;
double a = -5.42, b = 6.72;
//Print a, b, x, y
print("\na = $a b = $b x = $x y = $y");
//Truth table of OR and AND
print("\nBoolean AND (&&) Truth Table:");
print("false && false: ${false && false}");
print("false && true: ${false && true}");
print("true && false: ${true && false}");
print("true && true: ${true && true}");
print("\nBoolean OR (||) Truth Table:");
print("false || false: ${false || false}");
print("false || true: ${false || true}");
print("true || false: ${true || false}");
print("true || true: ${true || true}");
//Print results of logial operations
print("\n(a < b) || (b > x) : ${(a < b) || (b > x)}");
print("(x != y) && (a == b) : ${(x != y) && (a == b)}");
print("!(x >= y) : ${!(x >= y)}");
print("(true && (false || true)) : ${(true && (false || true))} ");
print("false || (true && !false) : ${false || (true && !false)} ");
print("(5 is double) && (4.3 is int) : ${(5 is double) && (4.3 is int)} ");
print("true && (12 is !String) && (a <= b) || (x != y) : ${true && (12 is !String) && (a <= b) || (x != y)}");
```

}
Output:

```
F:\Dart>dart run logicaloperators.dart

a = -5.42 b = 6.72 x = 23 y = 66

Boolean AND (&&) Truth Table:
false && false: false
false && true: false
true && false: false
true && true: true

Boolean OR (||) Truth Table:
false || false: false
false || true: true
true || false: true
true || true: true

(a < b) || (b > x) : true
(x != y) && (a == b) : false
!(x >= y) : true
(true && (false || true)) : true
false || (true && !false) : true
(5 is double) && (4.3 is int) : false
true && (12 is !String) && (a <= b) || (x != y) : true

F:\Dart>
```

9.5 Bitwise operators

Bitwise operators work on the individual bits of the operands. To understand this category of operators, some knowledge of boolean algebra and binary number system is needed.

Operator	Description	Sample Usage	Explanation
&	Bitwise Logical AND	x & y	Performs bitwise logical **AND**.
|	Bitwise Logical OR	x | y	Performs bitwise logical **OR**.
^	Bitwise Logical XOR	x ^ y	Performs bitwise logical **XOR**.
~	Bitwise Complement	~x	Computes 1's complement .
<<	Left Shift	x << y	Bits of left operand will be left shifted by the number of times specified by the right operand. For example, *x << 1* will left shift *x's* bits *1 time*.

41

>>	Right Shift	x >> y	Bits of left operand will be right shifted by the number of times specified by the right operand. For example, *y >> 3* will right shift *y's* bits *3 times*.

We will now write a Dart program to demonstrate the usage of bitwise operators. We will be using **<int variable>.toRadixString(2)** function from the **dart:core** library to print the binary equivalent of a number. In order to use this function, dart:core library should be imported as follows:

//The following statement should be the first line of code.
import 'dart:core';

Here is the program:

```
//Bitwise operators demo
//Import dart:core library to use toRadixString function
import 'dart:core';
//Mandatory main function of a Dart program
void main() {
//Declare some variables
int a = 6, b = 13, c = 4, d = 15;
//Print a b c and d in decimal as well as binary
print("\nDecimal equivalnet of variables (Base 10):");
print("\na = $a \tb = $b \tc = $c \td = $d");
print("\nBinary equivalnet of variables (Base 2):");
print("\na = ${a.toRadixString(2)} b = ${b.toRadixString(2)} c = ${c.toRadixString(2)} d = ${d.toRadixString(2)}");
print("\na | b : ${(a | b).toRadixString(2)}");
print("\nb & d : ${(b & d).toRadixString(2)}");
print("\nc ^ a : ${(c ^ a).toRadixString(2)}");
print("\n~d : ${(~d).toRadixString(2)}");
print("\na << 3 : ${(a << 3).toRadixString(2)}");
print("\nd >> 1 : ${(d >> 1).toRadixString(2)}");
}
```

Output:

```
F:\Dart>dart run bitwiseoperators.dart
Decimal equivalnet of variables (Base 10):
a = 6    b = 13   c = 4    d = 15
Binary equivalnet of variables (Base 2):
a = 110 b = 1101 c = 100 d = 1111
a | b : 1111
b & d : 1101
c ^ a : 10
~d : -10000
a << 3 : 110000
d >> 1 : 111
F:\Dart>
```

9.6 Assignment operators

The default assignment operator in Dart is given by the equal to sign (=) which assigns the value from right to the operand on the left. There are a few more assignment operators which perform compound assignment operations.

Operator	Description	Sample Usage	Equivalent To
+=	Perform addition, then assign sum to the operand on the left.	x += y	x = x + y
-=	Subtract operand on the right from the operand on the left and assign difference to the operand on the left.	x -= y	x = x – y
*=	Multiply operands and assign product to the operand on the left.	x *= y	x = x * y
/=	Divide the operand on the left by the operand on the	x /= y	x = x / y

	right and assign quotient to the operand on the left.		
~/=	Perform integer division and assign integer quotient to the operand on the left.	x ~/ = y	x = x ~/ y
%=	Divide the operand on the left by the operand on the right and assign the remainder to the operand on the left.	x %= y	x = x % y
&=	Perform Bitwise Logical AND, assign result to the operand on the left.	x &= y	x = x & y
|=	Perform Bitwise Logical OR, assign result to the operand on the left.	x |= y	x = x | y
^=	Perform Bitwise Logical XOR, assign result to the operand on the left.	x ^= y	x = x ^ y
<<=	Perform left shift, assign result to the operand on the left.	x <<= y	x = x << y
>>=	Perform right shift, assign result to the operand on the left.	x >>= y	x = x >> y

Here is a program that demonstrates the usage of these assignment operators:

```
//Forming expression using arithmetic operators
//Mandatory main function
void main() {
//Declare some variables
double a = 3.65, b = 5.32, c = -2.12, d = 8.44;
int x = 29, y = 13;
print("\na = $a b = $b c = $c d = $d\nx = $x y = $y");
a += b;
print("\nAfter performing a += b:\na = $a b = $b");
c -= d;
print("\nAfter performing c -= d:\nc = $c d = $d");
d *= b;
print("\nAfter performing d *= b:\nd = $d b = $b");
```

```
b /= a;
print("\nAfter performing b /= a:\nb = $b a = $a");
x ~/= y;
print("\nAfter performing x ~/= y: \nx = $x y = $y");
x <<= 3;
print("\nAfter performing x <<= 3:\nx = $x");
y >>= 1;
print("\nAfter performing y >>= 1:\ny = $y");
y |= 9;
print("\nAfter performing y |= 9: \nx = $x y = $y");
x ^= 4;
print("\nAfter performing x ^= 4: \nx = $x y = $y");
x &= 5;
print("\nAfter performing x &= 5: \nx = $x y = $y");
}
```

Output:

```
F:\Dart>dart run assignmentoperators.dart

a = 3.65 b = 5.32 c = -2.12 d = 8.44
x = 29 y = 13

After performing a += b:
a = 8.97 b = 5.32

After performing c -= d:
c = -10.559999999999999 d = 8.44

After performing d *= b:
d = 44.9008 b = 5.32

After performing b /= a:
b = 0.5930880713489409 a = 8.97

After performing x ~/= y:
x = 2 y = 13

After performing x <<= 3:
x = 16

After performing y >>= 1:
y = 6

After performing y != 9:
x = 16 y = 15

After performing x ^= 4:
x = 20 y = 15

After performing x &= 5:
x = 4 y = 15

F:\Dart>_
```

10. User Input

In this chapter, we will learn to build Dart console applications to interact with the user. All the programming examples that we have seen so far had hard coded variable values. Now, we will see how to accept input from the user.

We will be using **readLineSync()** function of the **Stdin** class from the **dart:io** package. Hence, a program that makes use of this function should import dart:io package using the following statement:

import 'dart:io';

The readLineSync funtion reads input from the standard input stream (**stdin**). In most cases, for console based applications, the standard input stream is the keyboard. Here is the general syntax:

String? <variable> = stdin.readLineSync();
Example:
String? Name = stdin.readLineSync();

This function implements a **blocking I/O call**. When the execution control encounters **readLineSync**, the execution of the program will pause allowing the user an opportunity to enter something through the keyboard. When the user does so (and presses Enter), whatever has been entered will be fetched and returned in string format to the variable marked by **<variable>** in the above code snippet. An important thing to note here is that the designated variable which will receive the returned value should be made **null safe** and hence, **question mark symbol (?)** should be appended to its data type during declaration(**String?** in this case).

Note: Since readLineSync implements a blocking I/O call, if the user does not enter anything at all, the execution will pause indefinitely and the program will keep on running unless it is terminated externally.

Let us consider a programming example where we will ask the user to enter something and print it back:

```
//User Input Demo using readLineSync function
//Need to import dart:io to use readLineSync
import 'dart:io';
//Mandatory main function
void main() {
//Prompt the user to enter something
print("\nEnter some text: ");
//Read using readLineSync function, store the returned value in text variable
//Declare a null safe variable to store user input
String? text = stdin.readLineSync();
//Print text
print("\nYou have entered: $text \n");
}
```

Output:

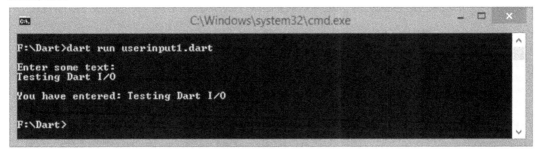

Let us take another programming example where we will ask the user to enter multiple values one by one:

```
//User Input Demo using readLineSync function
//Need to import dart:io to use readLineSync
import 'dart:io';
//Mandatory main function
void main() {
//Prompt the user to enter something
print("\nEnter your first name: ");
//Read using readLineSync function, store the returned value in first_name variable
//Declare a null safe variable to store user input
String? first_name = stdin.readLineSync();
print("\nEnter your last name: ");
//Read using readLineSync function, store the returned value in last_name variable
//Declare a null safe variable to store user input
```

```
String? last_name = stdin.readLineSync();
print("\nEnter your country: ");
//Read using readLineSync function, store the returned value in country variable
//Declare a null safe variable to store user input
String? country = stdin.readLineSync();
//Print everything
print("\nYou are $first_name $last_name and you are from $country. \n");
}
```

Output:

10.1 Reading numbers

The readLineSync function returns the entered value in a string format. Even if a number is entered, it will return in string format. This can present a problem in some cases. For example, if we want to read numbers from the user to perform mathematical operations, we will not be able to do so unless we somehow convert the numbers in string format to numeric format. To solve this problem, we can parse the number in string format to convert it to integer format using a function called ***int.parse***. Here is a general syntax:

String? <num in string> = stdin.readLineSync();
int <variable> = int.parse(<num in string>!);
Example:
String? num_str = stdin.readLineSync();
int num = int.parse(num_str!);

49

It is possible to call stdin.readLineSync from int.parse function which will read and parse in a single statement. Here is how to do it:

int? <variable> = int.parse(stdin.readLineSync()!);
Example:
int? num = int.parse(stdin.readLineSync()!);

Note: The combination of ? and ! Is used to make this process null safe.

Let us write a program to add two numbers which will be read from the user:

```
//User Input Demo - Read numbers using readLineSync and int.parse
//Need to import dart:io to use readLineSync

import 'dart:io';
//Mandatory main function
void main() {
//Prompt the user to enter something
print("\nEnter a number: ");
//Read using readLineSync function, store the returned number in num1_str variable as string
//Declare a null safe variable to store user input
String? num1_str = stdin.readLineSync();
//Parse num1_str to convert from string to int
//Add ! at the end of num1_str to make it null safe
int num1 = int.parse(num1_str!);
print("\nEnter another number: ");
/*Call stdin.readLineSync() from int.parse
This will pass the value read using readLineSync to int.parse
Add ! at the end of readLineSync() to make it null safe
*/
int? num2 = int.parse(stdin.readLineSync()!);
//Add num1 and num2, store in sum
int sum = num1 + num2;
//Print sum
print("\nSum of $num1 and $num2 is $sum \n");
}
```

Output:

Instead of reading integers, if you would like to read double values, you can use **double.parse** function instead of **int.parse**. Here is a programming example where we read two double values from the user, divide them and print the quotient:

```dart
//User Input Demo - Read double using readLineSync and double.parse
//Need to import dart:io to use readLineSync
import 'dart:io';
//Mandatory main function
void main() {
//Prompt the user to enter something
print("\nEnter a number (double): ");
//Read using readLineSync function, store the returned number in num1_str variable as string
//Declare a null safe variable to store user input
String? num1_str = stdin.readLineSync();
//Parse num1_str to convert from string to double
//Add ! at the end of num1_str to make it null safe
double num1 = double.parse(num1_str!);
print("\nEnter another number (double): ");
/*Call stdin.readLineSync() from int.parse
This will pass the value read using readLineSync to int.parse
Add ! at the end of readLineSync() to make it null safe
*/
double? num2 = double.parse(stdin.readLineSync()!);
//Divide num1 and num2, store quotient in quotient
double quotient = num1 / num2;
//Print quotient
print("\n$num1 / $num2 = $quotient \n");
}
```

Output:

11. Decision Making

Decision making constructs are programming control structures which introduce conditionality or branching in programming. All the programs that we have learnt so far had a linear way of execution. That is, a program would start executing from the first line of the code till the last one. Using decision making constructs, we can alter this linear way of execution. Dart offers **if-else** and **switch-case** constructs for decision making.

11.1 if-else construct

The if-else construct is the simplest option available for decision making. This can be realized using a single if construct. Here is the general syntax:

```
if (<condition>) {
//if-block begins
//Statements to be executed if <condition> is true.
...
...
...
//if-block ends
}
Example:
if (age > 17) {
print("\nYou are an adult.");
}
```

The if statement accepts a condition marked by **<condition>** in the above code snippet. This <condition> is in most cases a boolean expression that can evaluate to either **true** or **false**. If it evaluates to true, the statements inside the if-block (code enclosed within curly brackets {}) will be executed one by one. If the condition evaluates to false, the statements inside the block will not be executed and the execution control will move to the statement (if present) after the if-block.

Let us write a simple program to read a number from the user and check if it is greater than 10:

```
//if demo
//Need to import dart:io to use readLineSync
import 'dart:io';
//Mandatory main function
void main() {
//Prompt the user to enter something
print("\nEnter a number: ");
//Read using readLineSync function, store the returned number in num1_str variable as string
//Declare a null safe variable to store user input
String? num1_str = stdin.readLineSync();
//Parse num1_str to convert from string to int
//Add ! at the end of num1_str to make it null safe
int num1 = int.parse(num1_str!);
//Check if num is greater than 10
if ( num1 > 10 ) {
print("\n$num1 is greater than 10.\n");
}
}
```

Output:

During the above run, we enter 77 and the application rightly points out that 77 is greater than 10. Let us now enter a value less than 10 and see what happens:

54

We entered 5 this time and the program exited quietly. This is because, a single if construct will only execute the block if the given condition is true, if it is false, the program will skip the block and continue executing the remaining statements. Since there are no statements after the if block, the program quits. If we want to handle the situation when the given condition evaluates to false, we need to include an else block immediately following the if-block. Here is the general syntax:

```
if (<condition>) {
//if-block begins
//Statements to be executed if <condition> is true.

...

...

...
//if-block ends
}
else {
//else block begins here
//Statements to be executed if <condition> is false.

...

...

...
//else block ends here
}
Example:
if (age > 17) {
print("\nYou are an adult.");
```

}
else {
print("\nYou are not an adult.");
}

Let us modify the previous program to handle the situation when the user enter a value less than 10:

```dart
//if-else demo
//Need to import dart:io to use readLineSync
import 'dart:io';
//Mandatory main function
void main() {
//Prompt the user to enter something
print("\nEnter a number: ");
//Read using readLineSync function, store the returned number in num1_str variable as string
//Declare a null safe variable to store user input
String? num1_str = stdin.readLineSync();
//Parse num1_str to convert from string to int
//Add ! at the end of num1_str to make it null safe
int num1 = int.parse(num1_str!);
//Check if num1 is greater than 10
if ( num1 > 10 ) {
print("\n$num1 is greater than 10.\n");
}
//If num1 is not greater than 10, the following else block will be executed
else {
print("\n$num1 is less than 10.\n");
}
}
```

Output:

```
F:\Dart>dart run ifelsedemo.dart

Enter a number:
52

52 is greater than 10.

F:\Dart>dart run ifelsedemo.dart

Enter a number:
3

3 is less than 10.

F:\Dart>
```

As seen from the above example, one combination of if-else blocks will let you test for one condition. Do something if the condition is met and do something else if the condition is not met. There is another construct called **else if** with the help of which, we can test for multiple conditions. Each else if statement can have a condition of its own. Here is a general syntax:

if (<condition 1>) {
//Statements to be executed if <condition 1> is true
}
else if (<condition 2>) {
//Statements to be executed if <condition 1> if false and <condition 2> is true
}
else if (<condition 3>) {
//Statements to be executed if <condition 1> and <condition 2> are false and <condition 3> is true
}
...
...
...
else if (<condition n>) {
//Statements to be executed if <condition 1> to <condition (n-1)> are false and <condition n> is true

```
}
else {
//Statements to be executed if none of the conditions are true
}
```

There needs to be a mandatory if block for an else if block to work. If the condition of the if block does not evaluate to true, the condition of the else if block will be checked; if that condition evaluates to true, the else if block will be executed. If not, the condition of the next else if block will be checked. This will go on happening until a true condition is found. If none of the conditions evaluate to true, then the else block (if it is present) will be executed.

Let us consider a programming example where we will check if the given number is positive, negative or zero:

```
//if-else if-else demo
//Need to import dart:io to use readLineSync
import 'dart:io';
//Mandatory main function
void main() {
//Prompt the user to enter something
print("\nEnter a number: ");
//Read using readLineSync function, store the returned number in num1_str variable as string
//Declare a null safe variable to store user input
String? num1_str = stdin.readLineSync();
//Parse num1_str to convert from string to int
//Add ! at the end of num1_str to make it null safe
int num1 = int.parse(num1_str!);
//Check if num1 is greater than 0, meaning positive
if ( num1 > 0 ) {
print("\n$num1 is positive.\n");
}
//Check if num1 is less than 0, meaning negative
else if ( num1 < 0 ) {
print("\n$num1 is negative.\n");
}
//If the number is neither positive, nor negative, means it is 0
else
{
print("\n$num1 is zero.\n");
```

```
}
}
```

Let us consider another example where we will ask the user to enter a number and check if it lies between 0-9, 10-19, ... 90-99 range:

```
//if-else if-else demo with logical operators
//Need to import dart:io to use readLineSync
import 'dart:io';
//Mandatory main function
void main() {
//Prompt the user to enter something
print("\nEnter a number: ");
//Read using readLineSync function, store the returned number in
num1_str variable as string
//Declare a null safe variable to store user input
String? num1_str = stdin.readLineSync();
```

```dart
//Parse num1_str to convert from string to int
//Add ! at the end of num1_str to make it null safe
int num1 = int.parse(num1_str!);
//Check in which range num1 falls
if ( (num1 >= 0) && (num1 < 10) ) {
print("\n$num1 is between 0 and 9.\n");
}
else if ( (num1 >= 10) && (num1 < 20) ) {
print("\n$num1 is between 10 and 19.\n");
}
else if ( (num1 >= 20) && (num1 < 30) ) {
print("\n$num1 is between 20 and 29.\n");
}
else if ( (num1 >= 30) && (num1 < 40) ) {
print("\n$num1 is between 30 and 39.\n");
}
else if ( (num1 >= 40) && (num1 < 50) ) {
print("\n$num1 is between 40 and 49.\n");
}
else if ( (num1 >= 50) && (num1 < 60) ) {
print("\n$num1 is between 50 and 59.\n");
}
else if ( (num1 >= 60) && (num1 < 70) ) {
print("\n$num1 is between 60 and 69.\n");
}
else if ( (num1 >= 70) && (num1 < 80) ) {
print("\n$num1 is between 70 and 79.\n");
}
else if ( (num1 >= 80) && (num1 < 90) ) {
print("\n$num1 is between 80 and 89.\n");
}
else if ( (num1 >= 90) && (num1 < 100) ) {
print("\n$num1 is between 90 and 99.\n");
}
```

```
//If the number does not come under any range
else
{
print("\n$num1 is either less than 0 or greater than 99.\n");
}
}
```

Output:

```
F:\Dart>dart run range.dart

Enter a number:
43

43 is between 40 and 49.

F:\Dart>dart run range.dart

Enter a number:
106

106 is either less than 0 or greater than 99.

F:\Dart>dart run range.dart

Enter a number:
75

75 is between 70 and 79.
```

Note:

- An if statement can be a stand-alone statement however an else if and else statements need a preceding if statement to work.

- A condition can only be specified for an if statement or an else if statement.

- Only else if blocks are permitted to be placed between an if block and an else block. No other statements are permitted.

- Only one block is executed in one if-else if-else block combination. If a condition evaluates to true, that particular block is executed and the remaining blocks are skipped even if their conditions would evaluate to true.

11.2 switch-case construct

We have seen that we can account for multiple conditions using multiple if - else if - else statements. However, there is even better way to do it using switch-case construct. Here is the general syntax:

```
switch (<expression>) {
case <constant expression 1>: { //Statement to be executed for const exp 1}
    break;
case <constant expression 2>: { //Statement to be executed for const exp 2}
    break;
case <constant expression 3>: { //Statement to be executed for const exp 3}
    break;
    ...
    ...
    ...
case <constant expression n>: { //Statement to be executed for const exp n}
    break;
default: { //Statement to be executed if there is no matching exp
}
}
```

A switch statement is given an expression, marked by **<expression>** in the above code snippet. Inside the switch block, there are multiple cases where each case statement has a constant expression of its own. The overall idea is that when the expression of the switch statement is evaluated, the resultant value must be present as a constant expression of one of the case blocks for it to be executed. This is how it works step by step – the expression of the switch statement is evaluated and a resultant value is obtained. This value will be checked against the constant expressions of each of the case blocks one by one. If a match is found, that particular case block is executed and if not, the next case statement's constant expression is checked. This is known as **testing for case**s. If no matching expression is found, the **default** block is executed. A **break** statement is used to halt the execution after a particular case block is executed; without it, the remaining cases will go on executing until either there are no more cases left or a break statement is encountered.

Let us write a program to ask the user to enter a digit from 0 to 9 and print its equivalent in words:

```
//switch demo
//Need to import dart:io to use readLineSync
import 'dart:io';
//Mandatory main function
void main() {
//Prompt the user to enter something
print("\nEnter a number (0-9): ");
//Read using readLineSync function, store the returned number in num1_str variable as string
//Declare a null safe variable to store user input
String? num1_str = stdin.readLineSync();
//Parse num1_str to convert from string to int
//Add ! at the end of num1_str to make it null safe
int num1 = int.parse(num1_str!);
switch (num1) {
case 0: { print("Zero"); }
break;
case 1: { print("One"); }
break;
case 2: { print("Two"); }
break;
case 3: { print("Three"); }
break;
case 4: { print("Four"); }
break;
```

```
case 5: { print("Five"); }
break;
case 6: { print("Six"); }
break;
case 7: { print("Seven"); }
break;
case 8: { print("Eight"); }
break;
case 9: { print("Nine"); }
break;
default: { print("$num1 is either less than 0 or greater than 9.\n"); }
}
}
```

Output:

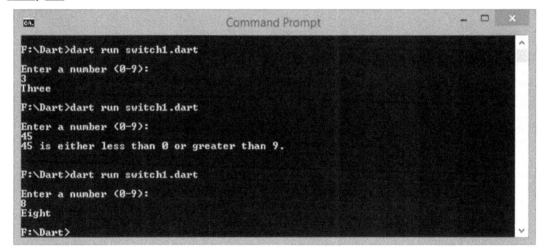

Let us consider another example to check whether a given alphabet is a vowel or a consonant. This example will also demonstrate the importance of the break statement:

```
//switch demo
//Need to import dart:io to use readLineSync
import 'dart:io';
//Mandatory main function
void main() {
//Prompt the user to enter something
print("\nEnter an alphabet: ");
//Read using readLineSync function, store the returned number in num1_str variable as
string
```

```
//Declare a null safe variable to store user input
String? input_str = stdin.readLineSync();
switch (input_str) {
case "a":
case "e":
case "i":
case "o":
case "u":
case "A":
case "E":
case "I":
case "O":
case "U": { print("\n$input_str is a vowel.\n"); }
break;
default: {print ("\n$input_str is a consonant.\n"); }
}
}
```

Output:

There is another way to write the switch-case construct and is a preferred way when there are multiple statements to be executed inside case blocks:

switch (<expression>) {
case <constant expression 1>:
/* Statements to be executed if
<expression> matches <constant expression 1>*/
break;
case <constant expression 2>:
/* Statements to be executed if
<expression> matches <constant expression 2>*/
break;
case <constant expression 3>:
/* Statements to be executed if
<expression> matches <constant expression 3>*/
break;

...
...
...
case <constant expression n>:
/* Statements to be executed if
<expression> matches <constant expression n>*/
break;
default:
//Statements to be executed if <expression> matches none of
the constant expressions
}

Let us write a program to read two numbers from the user and present a choice of addition, subtraction, multiplication and division:

```
//Switch Demo - menu driven program
//Need to import dart:io to use readLineSync
import 'dart:io';
//Mandatory main function
void main() {
```

```
//Prompt the user to enter something
print("\nEnter a number (double): ");
//Read using readLineSync function, store the returned number in num1_str variable as
string
//Declare a null safe variable to store user input
String? num1_str = stdin.readLineSync();
//Parse num1_str to convert from string to double
//Add ! at the end of num1_str to make it null safe
double num1 = double.parse(num1_str!);
print("\nEnter another number (double): ");
/*Call stdin.readLineSync() from int.parse
This will pass the value read using readLineSync to int.parse
Add ! at the end of readLineSync() to make it null safe
*/
double? num2 = double.parse(stdin.readLineSync()!);
//Print menu
print("\n1. Sum\n2. Difference\n3. Product\n4. Quotient\n\nChoice: ");
//Read choice
int? choice = int.parse(stdin.readLineSync()!);
//Switch according to users choice
switch(choice) {
case 1:
double sum = num1 + num2;
print("\n$num1 + $num2 = $sum");
break;
case 2:
double diff = num1 - num2;
print("\n$num1 - $num2 = $diff");
break;
case 3:
double prod = num1 * num2;
print("\n$num1 * $num2 = $prod");
break;
case 4:
double q = num1 / num2;
print("\n$num1 / $num2 = $q");
break;
default:
print("\nInvalid Choice!");
}
}
```

Output:

```
Command Prompt                                          _  □  ×

F:\Dart>dart run switch3.dart

Enter a number (double):
12.5

Enter another number (double):
31.8

1. Sum
2. Difference
3. Product
4. Quotient

Choice:
1

12.5 + 31.8 = 44.3

F:\Dart>dart run switch3.dart

Enter a number (double):
-56.12

Enter another number (double):
-31.48

1. Sum
2. Difference
3. Product
4. Quotient

Choice:
4

-56.12 / -31.48 = 1.7827191867852603

F:\Dart>_
```

12. Loops

Loops are control structures which facilitate the execution of a piece of code multiple times over as long as a certain condition is satisfied. Dart offers the following loops – *while* loop, *do while* loop, *for* loop, *for* in loop and *foreach* loop. In this section, we will learn while loop, do while loop and for loop. The remaining two loops are covered in the *Lists* chapter.

12.1 while loop

The general syntax of a while loop is:

```
while (<condition>) {
//Statements to be executed as long as <condition> evaluates to
true.
}
Example:
int count = 0;
while (count < 5) {
print("Hello!");
count++;
}
```

The while loop needs to be given a condition, marked by **<condition>** in the above code snippet. This condition is a boolean expression which can evaluate to either *true* or *false*. If the condition evaluates to false, the while loop will be skipped. If it evaluates to true, the statements inside the while block will be executed one by one till the last statement. One instance of a loop block execution is known as a loop *iteration*. Once end of block has been reached, the control will jump back to the while statement where the given condition will be checked again, if it evaluates to true again, the whole loop block will be executed again (2nd iteration). This process will go on happening as long as the condition keeps evaluating to true. Once it evaluates to false, the loop will no longer execute. If the condition never evaluates to false, the loop will go on executing indefinitely. Such a loop is known as an *infinite loop*. When an application has an infinite loop in it, the execution control will be stuck inside the loop and the application will go on running indefinitely unless terminated externally.

It is a good idea to use a loop variable to keep track of the iterations. In the above example, the variable **count** is used as a loop variable. It is initialized to 0 before entering the loop, incremented by one at the end of each iteration. The given condition is **count < 5**. That is, the loop will execute five times – from **count = 0** to **count = 4**. Let us write a simple program using while loop to print multiples of 2 from 2 to 20:

```
//while loop demo - multiple of 2
//Mandatory main function
void main() {
//Declare a loop variable, initialize to 1
var i = 1;
//Loop from 1 to 10
while (i < 11) {
//Print i x 2
print("${i * 2}");
//Increment i
i++;
}
}
```

Output:

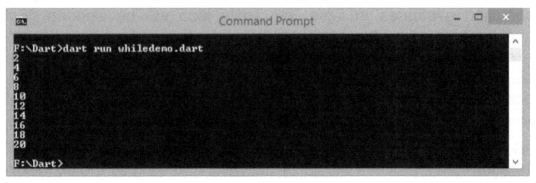

Note: It is easy to make mistakes when learning loops for the first time. You may unintentionally write infinite loops and your application may get stuck indefinitely. In such a case, press ***Ctrl + C*** to issue a keyboard interrupt and terminate the application.

12.2 Do While Loop

The do while loop works similar to the while loop. One major difference is that the condition is checked at the end of the loop block as opposed to at the beginning of the loop. As a result, this loop is guaranteed to execute at least once even if the given condition is false. Here is the general syntax:

do {
//Statements to be executed as long as <condition> is true.
} while (condition);
Example:
int count = 0;
do {
print(count);
count++;
} while (count < 10);

Let us write a program to evaluate the following function for the values of x from -5 to 5:

$$f(x) = 4x^2 - 3x + 5$$

```
//do while loop demo - evaluation of an expression
//Expression -> 4 * x * x - 3 * x + 5
//Mandatory main function
void main() {
//Declare a loop variable, initialize to -5
var x = -5;
//Loop from -5 to 5
do {
//Print i x 2
print("x = $x\tf(x) = ${((4 * x * x) - (3 * x) + 5)}");
//Increment x
x++;
```

```
} while (x < 6);
}
```

Output:

12.3 for loop

The for loop has more features as compared to while and do while loops. Loop variable initialization, specifying of condition and loop variable expression (increment, decrement, etc.) can be done in a single statement. Here is the general syntax:

> for (<loop var initialization>; <condition>; <expression>) {
> //Statements to be executed as long as <condition> is true
> }
> Example:
> for (int i = 10 ; i > 0 ; i --) {
> print ("${ i * 10} ");
> }

Let us write a program to calculate the factorial of a given number. The factorial of a number *n* is denoted by *n!* where *n! = n x (n – 1) x (n – 2) x ... x 1*. This can also be written using the recursive formula *n! = n x (n – 1)!*. For example, 5! = 5 x 4 x 3 x 2 x 1 = 120. Factorial of a negative number cannot be calculated and the factorial of 0 is 1. Here is the program:

//for loop demo - factorial

72

```dart
//Need to import dart:io to use readLineSync
import 'dart:io';
//Mandatory main function
void main() {
//Declare a variable to store factorial
int factorial = 1;
//Ask the user to enter a Number
print("\nEnter a number (integer): ");
int? num = int.parse(stdin.readLineSync()!);
//loop from 1 to num
for(int i = 1; i <= num ; i++) {
factorial = factorial * i;
}
print("\nFactorial of $num is $factorial.");
}
```

Output:

12.4 Loop control

All the above mentioned loops will go on executing as long as the given condition keeps evaluating to true. You can have more control over the execution of the loop using loop control statements. Dart offers two loop control statements – **break** and **continue**. The break statement will break the control out of the loop thereby terminating it even if the condition remains true. Where as, the continue statement will skip the current iteration and move to the next one. Let us understand the working of these statements using programming examples.

Here is a program that prints multiples of 3 from 3 to 57 but skips that number which is also a multiple of 5. In order to skip printing such a number, the continue statement is used:

```
//continue demo
//Mandatory main function
void main() {
//Declare a loop variable
int i = 1;
//loop from 1 to 20
while (i <= 20) {
//check if i * 3 is a multiple of 5
if ((i * 3) % 5 == 0){
i++;
continue;
}
print("${i * 3}");
i++;
}
}
```

Output:

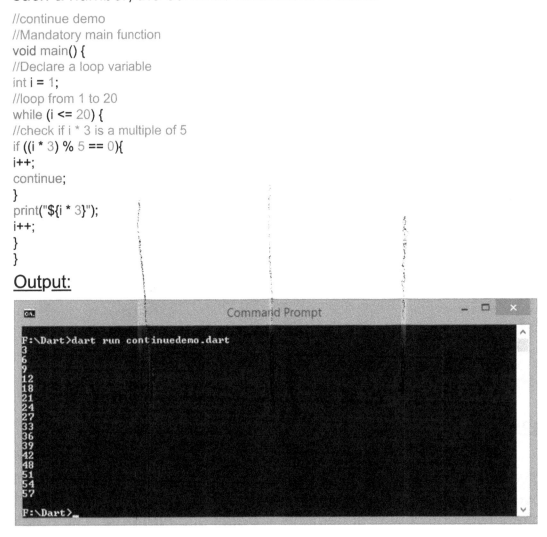

```
F:\Dart>dart run continuedemo.dart
3
6
9
12
18
21
24
27
33
36
39
42
48
51
54
57
F:\Dart>
```

Let us write a program to check whether a given number is prime or composite. A break statement is used to break out of the loop if the

74

given number is divisible by any other number:

```dart
//break demo -- prime or composite
//Need to import dart:io to use readLineSync

import 'dart:io';
//Mandatory main function
void main() {
//Use a boolean flag to keep a track of divisibility
bool isPrime = true;
//Ask the user to enter a number:
print("\nEnter a number (integer): ");
int? num = int.parse(stdin.readLineSync()!);
//Loop from 2 to num - 1
for (int i = 2 ; i < num ; i ++) {
if (num % i == 0) {
//If num is divisible, set isPrime to flase
isPrime = false;
//Break out of the loop
break;
}
}
if (isPrime) {
print("\n$num is prime.\n");
}
else {
print("\n$num is composite.\n");
}
}
```

Output:

Let us now combine whatever we have learned in decision making and loops chapter and write a menu driven program to calculate sum, difference, product and quotient of two numbers:

```
//Menu driven program with switch and while
//Need to import dart:io to use readLineSync
import 'dart:io';
//Mandatory main function
void main() {
int choice = 0;
while (choice != 5) {
print("\n1. Addition\n2. Subtraction\n3. Multiplication\n4. Division\n5. Quit\n\nChoice: ");
//Read choice
choice = int.parse(stdin.readLineSync()!);
//Switch according to users choice
switch(choice) {
case 1:
//Prompt the user to enter something
print("\nEnter a number (double): ");
//Read using readLineSync function, store the returned number in num1_str variable as string
//Declare a null safe variable to store user input
String? num1_str = stdin.readLineSync();
//Parse num1_str to convert from string to double
//Add ! at the end of num1_str to make it null safe
double num1 = double.parse(num1_str!);
print("\nEnter another number (double): ");
/*Call stdin.readLineSync() from int.parse
This will pass the value read using readLineSync to int.parse
Add ! at the end of readLineSync() to make it null safe
*/
double? num2 = double.parse(stdin.readLineSync()!);

double sum = num1 + num2;
print("\n$num1 + $num2 = $sum");
break;
case 2:
print("\nEnter a number (double): ");
double? num1 = double.parse(stdin.readLineSync()!);
print("\nEnter another number (double): ");
double? num2 = double.parse(stdin.readLineSync()!);
double diff = num1 - num2;
print("\n$num1 - $num2 = $diff");
break;
```

```
case 3:
print("\nEnter a number (double): ");
double? num1 = double.parse(stdin.readLineSync()!);
print("\nEnter another number (double): ");
double? num2 = double.parse(stdin.readLineSync()!);
double prod = num1 * num2;
print("\n$num1 * $num2 = $prod");
break;
case 4:
print("\nEnter a number (double): ");
double? num1 = double.parse(stdin.readLineSync()!);
print("\nEnter another number (double): ");
double? num2 = double.parse(stdin.readLineSync()!);
double q = num1 / num2;
print("\n$num1 / $num2 = $q");
break;
case 5:
print("\nQuitting...\n");
break;
default:
print("\nInvalid Choice!");
}
}
}
```

Output:

```
Command Prompt                                                    _ □ ×

F:\Dart>dart run menudriven.dart

1. Addition
2. Subtraction
3. Multiplication
4. Division
5. Quit

Choice:
3

Enter a number (double):
-3543.245

Enter another number (double):
-0.06434

-3543.245 * -0.06434 = 227.97238329999996

1. Addition
2. Subtraction
3. Multiplication
4. Division
5. Quit

Choice:
5

Quitting...

F:\Dart>
```

13. Functions

A function is a piece of reusable code that performs a task or a group of tasks. Functions are also known as methods, routines or sub-routines. We have used a few functions so far. In this chapter, we will learn to write our own functions. Before learning this topic, we need to understand the need for functions. So far, we have heavily used the print function to print something on the console. Someone has already written the logic of print function to interact with the output stream and place whatever we want to print correctly on the console. Imagine if we had to do all that every time we wanted to print something. Usage of functions is code re-usability at its best.

For the sake of understanding, the topic of functions can be broadly classified into two sub topics – *function definition* and *function call* (of course there are many more topics, the broad classification is done only for understanding purpose). If you understand the distinction between these two topics, this chapter will be a piece of cake!

In short, function definition is the actual piece of code which does some work where as a function call is used to invoke the function definition.

13.1 Function definition

As mentioned earlier, a function definition is the piece of code written to perform a task or a set of tasks. Here is the general syntax to define a function:

<return type> <function name> (<arguments>) {
//Function body
//Statements
//Core part of the function – logic
<optional return statement>

}

Here are the components of a function definition:

Function name

Function name is the name given to a function in order to identify it. The rules of naming a function are the same as naming a variable.

Arguments

A function can accept data in the form of arguments. When there are multiple arguments, they need to separated using commas.

Return type and return statement

A function can optionally return a value back to the calling function (eg. main function). If a function does return a value, the return type should be the same as the data type of the value returned. In case a function does not return any value, the return type to be used is *void*.

Let us define a function that does not accept any arguments and does not return any value:

```
void sayHello() {
print("I say hello!");
}
```

The name of the function is *sayHello*, the return type is *void* which means it does not return any value. Inside the definition, we see that there is only one print statement that prints "I say hello!".

13.2 Function call

A function definition is a piece of code that sits idle unless invoked. In order to invoke a function, a function call must be made. Here is the general syntax to call a function:

```
<function name>(<arguments>);
Example:
```

sayHello();

Let us write a function that does not accept any arguments and does not return any value. We will call this function from main:

```
//Functions demo
//Define your Function
void simpleFunction() {
print("\n--- Inside simpleFunction ---");
}
//Mandatory main function
void main() {
print("\n... Inside main function ...");
print("\n... Caling simpleFunction ...");
//Call simpleFunction
simpleFunction();
print("\n... Back to main function ...");
}
```

Output:

13.3 Function Arguments

Data can be sent to a function in the form of arguments (also known as parameters). These arguments are received inside variables local to the particular function. If there are multiple arguments, they need to be separated using commas. Here is an example:

void showData(int a, double b, String c) {

```
print("a = $a b = $b c = $c);
}
```

The **showData** function accepts 3 arguments – **int a, double b** and **String c**. Inside this function, there is only one print statement that prints the values of these variables. Now let us see how this function can be called:

```
showData(5, 6.2, "wow");
int x = 88;
int y = -0.43;
String s = "Demo";
showData(x, y, s);
```

As seen from the function calls, we need to pass arguments in the same order that they are defined. In the first function call where we pass **5, 6.2** and **"wow"**, _5 will be received in a, 6.2 will be received in b and "wow" will be received in c_.

Let us write a program to demonstrate the usage of function parameters:

```
//Functions demo -- pass arguments
//Define your Functions
void displaySomething(String msg) {
print("\nInside displaySomething function.");
print("\nArgument passed: " + msg);
}
void printSomething(String msg) {
print("\nInside printSomething function.");
print("\nArgument passed: " + msg);
}
//Mandatory main function
void main() {
print("\n... Inside main function ...");
//Call displaySomething, pass a string
displaySomething("hello!!!");
//Declare and initialize a string variable
String s = "Dart!!!";
//Call printSomething, pass s as argument
printSomething(s);
print("\n... Back to main function ...");
```

```
}
```

Output:

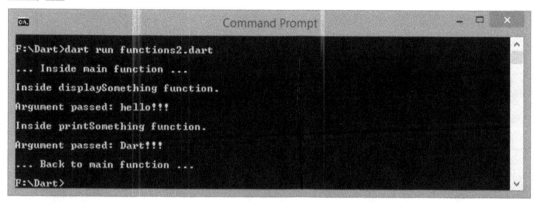

If you want to pass a value that has been read from the user, you will have to use null-safe variables. Here is a program that demonstrates just that:

```
//Functions demo -- pass nullsafe arguments
//Need to import dart:io to use readLineSync
import 'dart:io';
//Define your Function
/*displayMessage function accepts 1 argument of String? type
String? makes it null-safe. This is needed because we are passing
an argument which is read from the user
In such a case anything can go wrong when reading the input
Hence null safety is needed*/
void displayMessage(String? msg) {
print("\nInside displayMessage function.");
//While printing msg, ! must be appended at the end to make it null safe
print("\nYou have entered: " + msg!);
}
//Mandatory main function
void main() {
print("\n... Inside main function ...");
print("\nEnter somethig: ");
String? text = stdin.readLineSync();
```

```
print("\n... Caling displayMessage ... \nPassing text variable as argument.");
//Call simpleFunction
displayMessage(text);
print("\n... Back to main function ...");
}
```

Output:

Refer to the above program, inside main, we read a string from the user and store it in a String variable called text. This variable is defined as **String?** to make it null-safe. Inside the function definition, we need to receive it as **String?**. Hence, the variable **msg** has been declared as **String?**. Further, when we use the variable **msg**, we append **!** At the end.

13.4 Returning a value

A function can return a value back to the calling function using the return statement. Here is the general syntax:

return <value/variable/expression>;
Example:
return 10;
return (3/2);
*return (x * 5 + y);*

If a function returns a value, the return type needs to be specified in the function definition and it needs to be the same as data type of the value returned.

Let us write a program with two functions – add and subtract; accept two arguments each and return their sum and difference respectively:

```
//Return a value
//Function to add two numbers and return the sum
int add (int a, int b) {
//Declare a variable to store sum
int s = a + b;
//Return s
return s;
}
//Function to subtract two numbers and return the difference
int subtract (int a, int b) {
//Return a - b without storing a the difference in a variable
return (a - b);
}
//Mandatory main Function
void main() {
//Declare two variables and print them
int x = 16, y = 9;
print("\nx = $x\ty = $y");
//Declare sum and diff to store sum and difference respectively
int sum = add(x, y);
int diff = subtract(x, y);
//Print sum and diff
print("\nsum = $sum\ndiff = $diff\n");
}
```

Output:

```
F:\Dart>dart run functions4.dart
x = 16  y = 9

sum = 25
diff = 7

F:\Dart>
```

14. List

A list is a collection of items. Items in a list can be of the same data type or of different types depending on the type of the list. i.e., a list can be configured to hold items only of String type, int type, etc. or no data type can be specified for a list – such a list can hold items of different data types. The items inside a list are known as elements which can be accessed using their index. An index begins at 0 and ends at one less than the length of the list. For example, if there is a list of 5 elements, the first element will be present at index 0 and the last element will be present at index 4. Refer to the following image:

Elements =>	6.2	-9.5	8.1
Index =>	0	1	2

There is a list that holds elements of double type. We see 3 elements –> 6.2 (present at index 0), -9.5 (present at index 1) and 8.1 (present at index 2). Since the size of the list is 3, list indexes run from 0 to (3 – 1), that is 2.

Lists can be broadly classified in two categories – *fixed-length lists* and *growable lists*. As the names suggest, a fixed-length list has its maximum size defined at the time of declaration where as a growable list does not have its size defined at the time of declaration, it can even be empty. Elements can be added to a growable list as and when desired.

14.1 Fixed-length list

As mentioned before, the size of a fixed length list is determined at the time of declaration. Elements can neither be removed nor added to this type of a list. Also, such a list should be filled with an arbitrary value at the time of declaration. Here is a general syntax of declaring fixed-length lists:

var <list variable> = List<[data type]>.filled([list size], [initial value]);
Example:
//Create a list of type int, size 5, fill 0 at all locations
var x_list = List<int>.filled(5, 0);
//Create a list of type String, size 10, fill "Y" at all locations
var y_list = List<String>.filled(10, "Y");

The length of the list can be fetched using the length property as follows:

<list variable>.length
Example:
print("\nLength of x_list: ${x_list.length}");

Individual elements of a list can be accessed/updated using the [ ] operator as follows:

<list_variable>[<index>] = <expression>;
Example:
x_list[0] = 6;
x_list[3] = 9;
y_list[0] = "Hello";
y_list[1] = "Lists";

Let us write a Dart program to create a few lists, print their size, update the elements and print the updated lists:

```
//List Demo -- Fixed length lists
void main() {
//Declare a list of 5 elements of type double, fill 0.0
var lst_double = List<double>.filled(5, 0.0);
//Declare a list of 3 elements of type int, fill 0
var lst_int = List<int>.filled(3, 0);
//Declare a list of 4 elements of type String, fill 'A'
var lst_str = List<String>.filled(4, 'A');
```

```
//Print all lists
print("\nlst_double: $lst_double\nlst_double size: ${lst_double.length}");
print("\nlst_int: $lst_int\nlst_double size: ${lst_int.length}");
print("\nlst_str: $lst_str\nlst_double size: ${lst_str.length}");
//Change initial values of all lists
print("\nAfter updating lists:");
lst_double[0] = -4.5;
lst_double[1] = 6.9;
lst_double[2] = 0.1;
lst_double[3] = 2.5;
lst_double[4] = 9.2;
lst_int[0] = 63;
lst_int[1] = -36;
lst_int[2] = 41;
lst_str[0] = "This is";
lst_str[1] = "a List";
lst_str[2] = "programming";
lst_str[3] = "example";
//Print all lists again
print("\nlst_double: $lst_double\nlst_double size: ${lst_double.length}");
print("\nlst_int: $lst_int\nlst_int size: ${lst_int.length}");
print("\nlst_str: $lst_str\nlst_str size: ${lst_str.length}");
}
```

Output:

The elements of a list can even be printed directly with the help of their indexes. Here is an example:

```
//List Demo -- access element by element
void main() {
//Declare a list of 5 elements of type int, fill 0
var lst_int = List<int>.filled(5, 0);
//Update list elements by changing the values at indexes
lst_int[0] = 12;
lst_int[1] = -28;
lst_int[2] = 33;
lst_int[3] = -47;
lst_int[4] = 55;
//Print each list element by index
print("\nlst_int List:\nValue at index 0: ${lst_int[0]}");
print("\nValue at index 1: ${lst_int[1]}");
print("\nValue at index 2: ${lst_int[2]}");
print("\nValue at index 3: ${lst_int[3]}");
print("\nValue at index 4: ${lst_int[4]}");
}
```

Output:

```
F:\Dart>dart run lists2.dart

lst_int List:
Value at index 0: 12

Value at index 1: -28

Value at index 2: 33

Value at index 3: -47

Value at index 4: 55

F:\Dart>_
```

Since the length property fetches the length of the list, we can access the elements of a list using a loop where we can use a loop counter variable to iterate from 0 to length - 1. Here is an example where we use while loop to iterate through the loop:

```
//List Demo -- access element by element using loops
void main() {
//Declare a list of 7 elements of type int, fill 0
var lst_int = List<int>.filled(7, 0);
```

```
//Update list elements by changing the values at indexes
lst_int[0] = 345;
lst_int[1] = 432;
lst_int[2] = -120;
lst_int[3] = 605;
lst_int[4] = 134;
lst_int[5] = -289;
lst_int[6] = 718;
//Print each list element by index using while loop
int i = 0;
while ( i < lst_int.length ) {
print("\nValue at index $i: ${lst_int[i]}");
i++;
}
}
```

Output:

```
F:\Dart>dart run lists3.dart
Value at index 0: 345
Value at index 1: 432
Value at index 2: -120
Value at index 3: 605
Value at index 4: 134
Value at index 5: -289
Value at index 6: 718
F:\Dart>
```

14.2 Growable list

A growable list gives a lot more flexibility as compared to a fixed-length list. That is because, it is possible to add elements to a growable list as and when desired. Here is a general syntax to declare a growable list:

var <list variable> = <[Data Type]> [ ];
Example:
var list_1 = <int> [ ];
var list_2 = <double> [ ];

90

The above syntax will create an empty list. Some elements can be added at the time of declaration as follows:

var <list variable> = <[Data Type]> [(item 1), (item 2), ..., (item n)];

Example:
var list_3 = <int> [76, 12, -43, 23, 92];
var list_4 = <double> [-66.32, 12.54, 55.12];

A list can be defined to hold elements of different types by not specifying the data type as follows:

var <list variable> = [ ];
var <list variable> = [(item 1), (item 2), ... , (item n)];
Example:
var list_5 = [ ];
var list_6 = ["Fly", 56, "Butter", -12.7, true, "Cheese];

Elements to a growable list can be added using the **add** or **addAll** methods. Here is how to use the add method:

<list variable>.add(<item>);
Example:
list_3.add(47);
list_4.add(81.56);
list_5.add("aaa");
list_6.add(60);

Multiple elements can be added to a list using the addAll method as follows:

<list variable>.addAll({<item 1>, <item 2>,....});
Example:
list_3.add({1, 6, 3});
list_5.add({"ccc", 6.4, "aaa", false, 3});

Let us consider a programming example where we will define a few growable lists and add values to them:

//List Demo -- growable list

91

```
void main() {
//Declare an empty list
var lst1 = [];
//Declare a list of String type, add initial values
var lst2 = <String> ["Hello", "World"];
//Declare a list of int type, add initial values
var lst3 = <int> [6, -2, 8];
//Declare a generic list of different data types
var lst4 = ["ABC", -6.4, 0.65, 3, true, 55];
//Print lists
print("\nlst1: $lst1 \nlst1 length: ${lst1.length}");
print("\nlst2: $lst2 \nlst2 length: ${lst2.length}");
print("\nlst3: $lst3 \nlst3 length: ${lst3.length}");
print("\nlst4: $lst4 \nlst4 length: ${lst4.length}");
//Add values to all lists
lst1.add("Growable List!");
lst1.addAll({'Another element', 'ABC'});
lst2.add("!!!");
lst2.addAll({'...', '???'});
lst3.add(-3);
lst3.add(9);
lst3.addAll({-1, -5, 8});
lst4.add(false);
lst4.add(-3.56);
lst4.add("WOW!");
lst4.addAll({1, 3, 5});
//Print updated lists
print("\nUpdated Lists:");
print("\nlst1: $lst1 \nlst1 length: ${lst1.length}");
print("\nlst2: $lst2 \nlst2 length: ${lst2.length}");
print("\nlst3: $lst3 \nlst3 length: ${lst3.length}");
print("\nlst4: $lst4 \nlst4 length: ${lst4.length}");
}
```

Output:

```
Command Prompt                                              _ □ ✕

F:\Dart>dart run lists4.dart

lst1: []
lst1 length: 0

lst2: [Hello, World]
lst2 length: 2

lst3: [6, -2, 8]
lst3 length: 3

lst4: [ABC, -6.4, 0.65, 3, true, 55]
lst4 length: 6

Updated Lists:

lst1: [Growable List!, Another element, ABC]
lst1 length: 3

lst2: [Hello, World, !!!, ..., ???]
lst2 length: 5

lst3: [6, -2, 8, -3, 9, -1, -5, 8]
lst3 length: 8

lst4: [ABC, -6.4, 0.65, 3, true, 55, false, -3.56, WOW!, 1, 3, 5]
lst4 length: 12

F:\Dart>
```

14.3 for..in loop

In loops chapter, we skipped the ***for..in*** loop on purpose because it needs some knowledge of collections like lists. A for..in loop is used to iterate through a collection. Here is how to use it to iterate through a list:

for (var <variable> in <list variable>) {
//Statements
}
Example:
var list1 = [1, 5, 8, 3];
for (var x in list1) {
print(x);
}

During the first iteration of the loop, the first element of the list marked by ***<list variable>*** in the above code snippet will be fetched in the loop variable marked by ***<variable>***. During the second iteration, the second element will be fetched. This process will go on happening till the end of the list is reached. Here is a program that shows the working of a for..in loop:

```
//List Demo -- access element by element using for in loop
void main() {
//Declare a list of 5 elements of type int, fill 0
var lst_int = List<int>.filled(5, 0);
//Update list elements by changing the values at indexes
lst_int[0] = 12;
lst_int[1] = 43;
lst_int[2] = 61;
lst_int[3] = -33;
lst_int[4] = 89;
var lst_str = <String> ["Hello", "World", "!!!"];
//Print lst_int using for in loop
print("\nlst_int printed using for in loop: \n");
for (var value_int in lst_int) {
print(value_int);
}
print("\nlst_str printed using for in loop: \n");
for (var value_str in lst_str) {
print(value_str);
}
}
```

Output:

```
F:\Dart>dart run lists5.dart
lst_int printed using for in loop:

12
43
61
-33
89

lst_str printed using for in loop:

Hello
World
!!!

F:\Dart>
```

14.4 Properties of the List class

The List class has several properties. We have already seen how to use the length property. In this section, we will look at a few more:

isEmpty – returns true if the list is empty, returns false otherwise

isNotEmpty – returns false if the list is empty, returns true otherwise

length – returns the number of elements present in the list

first – returns the first element of the list

last – returns the last element of the list

single – returns true if the list has only one element, returns false otherwise

reversed – reverses the order of the elements

Let us write a program to check out these properties in action:

```
//List Demo -- list properties
void main() {
//Declare some lists
var lst1 = <int> [12, 75, 93];
var lst2 = [];
var lst3 = <double> [-5.2, -1.6, 8.3, -0.5, 9.1];
var lst4 = List<int>.filled(1, 0);
//Print all lists
```

95

```
print("\nlst1: $lst1 \nlst1 length: ${lst1.length}");
print("\nlst2: $lst2 \nlst2 length: ${lst2.length}");
print("\nlst3: $lst3 \nlst3 length: ${lst3.length}");
print("\nlst4: $lst4 \nlst4 length: ${lst4.length}");
//isEmpty  and  isNotEmpty
print("\nlst1.isEmpty - ${lst1.isEmpty}");
print("\nlst2.isEmpty - ${lst2.isEmpty}");
print("\nlst3.isNotEmpty - ${lst1.isNotEmpty}");
//first and last
print("\nlst1.first - ${lst1.first}");
print("\nlst3.last - ${lst3.last}");
//single
print("\nlst4.single - ${lst4.single}");
//reversed
print("\nlst1.reversed - ${lst1.reversed}");
print("\nlst3.reversed - ${lst3.reversed}");
print("\nlst4.reversed - ${lst4.reversed}");
}
```

Output:

```
F:\Dart>dart run lists6.dart

lst1: [12, 75, 93]
lst1 length: 3

lst2: []
lst2 length: 0

lst3: [-5.2, -1.6, 8.3, -0.5, 9.1]
lst3 length: 5

lst4: [0]
lst4 length: 1

lst1.isEmpty - false

lst2.isEmpty - true

lst3.isNotEmpty - true

lst1.first - 12

lst3.last - 9.1

lst4.single - 0

lst1.reversed - (93, 75, 12)

lst3.reversed - (9.1, -0.5, 8.3, -1.6, -5.2)

lst4.reversed - (0)

F:\Dart>_
```

14.5 Insert elements

Elements can be inserted into a growable list (and not a fixed-length list) using the **insert** or **insertAll** methods at a given location. Once inserted, the existing elements will be displaced to the right. Here is the general syntax:

<list variable>.insert(<index>, <element>);
<list variable>.insertAll(<index>, {<element 1>, <element 2>,
...});

Let us write a program to create a few growable lists and insert values into them:

```
//List Demo -- insert
void main() {
//Declare some lists
var lst1 = <int> [-1, -2, 9, 3, 6];
var lst2 = <double> [61.25, 72.31, 91.57];
```

97

```
//Print all lists
print("\nlst1: $lst1 \nlst1 length: ${lst1.length}");
print("\nlst2: $lst2 \nlst2 length: ${lst2.length}");
//Insert elements
lst1.insert(3, 0);
lst2.insertAll(1, {88.28, -54.76, 11.32, 97.91});
print("\nUpdated Lists:");
print("\nlst1: $lst1 \nlst1 length: ${lst1.length}");
print("\nlst2: $lst2 \nlst2 length: ${lst2.length}");
}
```

Output:

```
F:\Dart>dart run lists7.dart

lst1: [-1, -2, 9, 3, 6]
lst1 length: 5

lst2: [61.25, 72.31, 91.57]
lst2 length: 3

Updated Lists:

lst1: [-1, -2, 9, 0, 3, 6]
lst1 length: 6

lst2: [61.25, 88.28, -54.76, 11.32, 97.91, 72.31, 91.57]
lst2 length: 7

F:\Dart>
```

14.6 Search for an item

An item can be searched for inside a list using the ***indexOf*** and ***lastIndexOf*** functions. The indexOf function returns the index of the first occurrence of the item where as the lastIndexOf function returns the index of the last occurrence of the item. If the given item is not found, these functions return ***-1***. Here is the general syntax:

val location1 = <list variable>.indexOf(<item to be searched>);
val location2 = <list variable>.lastIndexOf(<item to be searched>);

Here is a program that demonstrates the usage of these functions:

```
//List Demo -- Search with - indexOf lastIndexOf
void main() {
```

98

```
//Declare some lists
var city_list = <String> ["Mumbai", "Singapore", "Perth", "Kyoto"];
var names = <String> ["Tiya", "Paul", "Gianna", "Paul", "Debby"];
var num = <int> [1, 2, 2, 3, 4, 1, 2, 5];
//Print all lists
print("\ncity: $city_list");
print("\nnames: $names");
print("\nnum: $num");
//Look for "Perth" in city_list
print("\nindexOf Perth in city_list: ${city_list.indexOf("Perth")}");
//Look for "Paul in names"
print("\nindexOf Paul in names: ${names.indexOf("Paul")}");
print("\nlastIndexOf Paul in names: ${names.lastIndexOf("Paul")}");
//Look for Seoul in city_list
print("\nindexOf Seoul in city_list: ${city_list.indexOf("Seoul")}");
//Look for 3 in num
print("\nindexOf 3 in num: ${num.indexOf(3)}");
//Look for 2 in num
print("\nindexOf 2 in num: ${num.indexOf(2)}");
print("\nindexOf 2 in num: ${num.lastIndexOf(2)}");
//Use indexOf to check if an element is present in a list
//Look for Mumbai in city_list
if (city_list.indexOf("Mumbai") != -1) {
print("\nMumbai is present in city_list");
}
else {
print("\nMumbai is NOT present in city_list");
}
//Look for Tokyo in city_list
if (city_list.indexOf("Tokyo") != -1) {
print("\Tokyo is present in city_list");
}
else {
print("\nTokyo is NOT present in city_list");
}
}
```

Output:

```
F:\Dart>dart run lists8.dart
city: [Mumbai, Singapore, Perth, Kyoto]
names: [Tiya, Paul, Gianna, Paul, Debby]
num: [1, 2, 2, 3, 4, 1, 2, 5]
indexOf Perth in city_list: 2
indexOf Paul in names: 1
lastIndexOf Paul in names: 3
indexOf Seoul in city_list: -1
indexOf 3 in num: 3
indexOf 2 in num: 1
indexOf 2 in num: 6
Mumbai is present in city_list
Tokyo is NOT present in city_list
F:\Dart>
```

14.7 Remove an item

An item can be removed from a growable list using the ***remove*** and ***removeAt*** functions. The remove function can be used to remove by item where as the removeAt function can be used to remove an item a particular location (index). Once the given item is removed, the remaining elements will be displaced to the left. Here is the general syntax:

<list variable>.remove<item to be removed>);

<list variable>.removeAt(<index of the item to be removed>);

Here is a program that demonstrates the working of these two functions:

```
//List Demo -- remove and removeAt
void main() {
//Declare some lists
var city = <String> ["Dubai", "Amman", "Bahrain"];
var num = <int> [6, 1, 9, 0, 2];
print("\ncity: $city");
print("\nnum: $num");
city.remove("Amman");
```

```
num.removeAt(4);
print("\nUpdated Lists:");
print("\ncity: $city");
print("\nnum: $num");
}
```

Output:

```
F:\Dart>dart run lists9.dart
city: [Dubai, Amman, Bahrain]
num: [6, 1, 9, 0, 2]
Updated Lists:
city: [Dubai, Bahrain]
num: [6, 1, 9, 0]
F:\Dart>
```

15. Map

A map is a data structure where data is stored as **key-value** pairs (also known as **KV** pairs). For each key, there is exactly one corresponding value. The keys are unique, values can be anything. Dart offers three main types of maps – **HashMap**, **LinkedHashMap** and **SplayTreeMap.** Out of these, we will learn HashMap and LinkedHashMap. SplayTreeMap is based on self-balancing binary trees, an advanced data structures concept and is beyond the scope of this book.

In the previous chapter, we learned Lists in great detail. Elements in a list are placed at indexes. Consider keys in a map as meaningful indexes and values as elements. Consider the following map used to store details of a person:

Map - person_data

There are 3 keys – **name**, **city** and **country** and there are exactly 3 values corresponding to each of these keys – **Junaid**, **Dubai** and **UAE**.

15.1 HashMap

A HashMap is an unordered map. That is, there is no guarantee that the key-value pairs will follow the order of insertion. Here is the general syntax to define a HashMap:

Map [<key data type>, <value data type>] [map variable] = HashMap();
Example:
Map <int, String> x = HashMap();

Note: Map and **HashMap()** are part of **dart:core** and **dart:collection** libraries respectively. Hence the dart:collection library must be included to use HashMap(). There is no need to included dart:core library as it is implicitly imported.

Once a HashMap is created, key-value pairs can be added on-the-fly. Here is the general syntax:

<map variable>[<key>] = <value>;
Example:
x[1] = "Dart";
x[2] = "book";

Note: The number of key-value pairs present in a map can be retrieved using the length property. For example, x.length will return the size of x.

The Map data structure is quiet versatile, the way you use it is up to you. You can use it to store many details of one entity or one detail of many entities, etc. Here is a program that has two maps. The first map stores different personal details of a person while the second map stores ages of different people:

```dart
//HashMap is a part of daty:collection library
import 'dart:collection';
//Mandatory main function
void main() {
//Create a Map to store the record of a person
Map<String, String> person = HashMap();
//Add   entries
person['firstName'] = "Irwin";
person['lastName'] = "Williams";
person['city'] = "Manchester";
person['country'] = "UK";
```

```dart
//Create another map to store the ages of different people
Map<String, int> age_person = HashMap();
age_person['Ronny'] = 23;
age_person['Bella'] = 21;
age_person['Fiona'] = 32;
age_person['Earl'] = 26;
age_person['Lilly'] = 29;
//Print both maps
print("\nperson Map:\n$person\nperson size: ${person.length}\n\nage_person Map:
\n$age_person\nage_person size: ${age_person.length}");
}
```

Output:

```
F:\Dart>dart run mapdemo.dart

person Map:
{country: UK, firstName: Irwin, city: Manchester, lastName: Williams}
person size: 4

age_person Map:
{Ronny: 23, Earl: 26, Fiona: 32, Bella: 21, Lilly: 29}
age_person size: 5

F:\Dart>
```

If you notice, the order of the insertion of key-value pairs is not followed when the contents of the maps are printed.

15.2 LinkedHashMap

A LinkedHashMap is an ordered Map. That is, the iteration will happen in the insertion order of the key-value pairs. Here is the general syntax of declaring a LinkedHashMap:

Map [<key data type>, <value data type>] [map variable] = LinkedHashMap();

Example:

Map <String, int> y = LinkedHashMap();

Note: LinkedHashMap() is part the **dart:collection** library. Hence it must be imported in every program that makes use LinkedHashMap;

104

Other than the order being preserved in a linked hash map, there is no major difference. It behaves like any other map (eg. HashMap). Let us write a program to demonstrate how does a LinkedHashMap work:

```dart
//LinkedHashMap is a part of daty:collection library
import 'dart:collection';
//Mandatory main function
void main() {
//Create a Map to store the record of a person
Map<String, String> person = LinkedHashMap();
//Add   entries
person['firstName'] = "Irwin";
person['lastName'] = "Williams";
person['city'] = "Manchester";

person['country'] = "UK";
//Create another map to store the ages of different people
Map<String, int> age_person = LinkedHashMap();
age_person['Ronny'] = 23;
age_person['Bella'] = 21;
age_person['Fiona'] = 32;
age_person['Earl'] = 26;
age_person['Lilly'] = 29;
//Print both maps
print("\nperson Map:\n$person\n\nage_person Map: \n$age_person");
}
```

Output:

```
F:\Dart>dart run linkedmapdemo.dart

person Map:
{firstName: Irwin, lastName: Williams, city: Manchester, country: UK}

age_person Map:
{Ronny: 23, Bella: 21, Fiona: 32, Earl: 26, Lilly: 29}

F:\Dart>
```

As seen from the output, when the contents of LinkedHashMap are printed, it happens in the same order that was followed during insertion.

15.3 Iterate using forEach method

The Map class has a ***forEach*** method which is very useful for iterating through a map. Here is how to use this function:

<map variable>.forEach((key, value) {
//Statements
});
Example:
Map <int, String> x = LinkedHashMap();
x[1] = 'one';
x[2] = 'two';
x[3] = 'three';
x[4] = 'four';
x.forEach((key, value) {
print("$key \t $value);
  });

In the above example, the Map x contains four KV pairs. When the control enters the forEach block, the first KV pair will be fetched during the first iteration where 1 will be received in the variable key and 'one' will be received in the variable value. This will go on happening will the last KV pair is fetched. Let us write a program to store weekdays where the key will be the serial number of the day and the value will be the name of the day:

```
//Map Demo -- forEach
//HashMap is a part of daty:collection library
import 'dart:collection';
//Mandatory main function
void main() {
//Declare a HashMap called days to store days of the week
//Key will be Sr. No. (int), and the name of the day will be the value (String)
Map<int, String> days = HashMap();
//Add entries
//Use [] operatory
days[1] = "Sunday";
days[2] = "Monday";
days[3] = "Tuesday";
```

```dart
days[4] = "Wednesday";
days[5] = "Thursday";
days[6] = "Friday";
days[7] = "Saturday";
//Print days
print("\nDays Map: \n$days");
//Print using forEach
print("\nIterating days using forEach:\n");
days.forEach((key, value) {
print("Key: $key Value: $value");
});
}
```

Output:

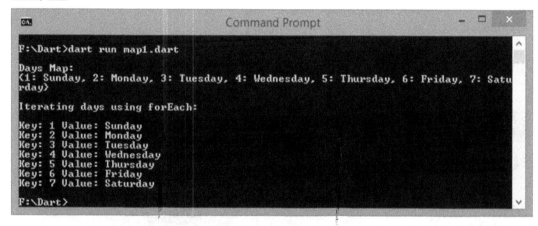

If you do not want to use the forEach method, you can always access KV pairs using their keys. This is fine for small maps but for larger ones, this method will be cumbersome. Here is an example:

```dart
//Map Demo -- print KV pairs using keys
//Map class is a part of dart:core library
//LinkedHashMap is a part of daty:collection library
import 'dart:collection';
import 'dart:core';
//Mandatory main function
void main() {
//Declare a LinkedHashMap called days to store days of the week
//Key will be the name of the day (String) ans Sr. No. (int), and will be the value
Map<String, int> days = LinkedHashMap();
//Add entries
//Use [] operatory
```

```
days['sunday'] = 1;
days['monday'] = 2;
days['tuesday'] = 3;
days['wednesday'] = 4;
days['thursday'] = 5;
days['friday'] = 6;
days['saturday'] = 7;
//Print one by one
print("\ndays Map:\n");
print("Key: sunday \t Value: ${days['sunday']}");
print("Key: monday \t Value: ${days['monday']}");
print("Key: tuesday \t Value: ${days['tuesday']}");
print("Key: wednesday \t Value: ${days['wednesday']}");
print("Key: thursday \t Value: ${days['thursday']}");
print("Key: friday \t Value: ${days['friday']}");
print("Key: saturday \t Value: ${days['saturday']}");
}
```

Output:

15.4 Add elements using addAll and addEntries methods

We have seen that a new KV pair can be added by specifying its key inside the [ ] operator and its corresponding value on the right hand side. In this section, we will see how to add elements using addAll and addEntries methods. Here is the general syntax:

//addAll syntax

108

<map variable>.addAll({<key 1>: <value 1>, <key 2>: <value 2>, ...
<key n>: <value n>});
//addEntries syntax
//Create an entry first
var <entry var> = <[key data type], [value data type]> {<key 1>:
<value 1>, <key n>: <value n>};
//Add entry
<map variable>.addEntries(<entry var>.entries);

Here is a program that demonstrates how these two methods work:

```
//Map Demo -- addAll and addEntries
//HashMap is a part of daty:collection library
import 'dart:collection';
//Mandatory main function
void main() {
//Declare a HashMap called days to store months
Map<String, int> months = LinkedHashMap();
//Add entries
//Use [] operatory
months['january'] = 1;
months['february'] = 2;
months['march'] = 3;
//Add 1 entry using addAll
months.addAll({'april': 4});
//Add multiple entries using addAll
months.addAll({'may': 5, 'june': 6, 'july': 7, 'august': 8});
//Add entry using addEntries
//Create a key-value pair as an entry
var month_9 = <String, int> {'september': 9};
//Add month_9 to months map
months.addEntries(month_9.entries);
//Create multiple key value pairs and add to months map
var month_10_to_12 = <String, int> {'october': 10, 'november': 11, 'december': 12};
months.addEntries(month_10_to_12.entries);
//Print months map using forEach
months.forEach((key, value) {
print("Key: $key \t Value: $value");
});
}
```

Output:

```
F:\Dart>dart run map3.dart
Key: january     Value: 1
Key: february    Value: 2
Key: march       Value: 3
Key: april       Value: 4
Key: may         Value: 5
Key: june        Value: 6
Key: july        Value: 7
Key: august      Value: 8
Key: september   Value: 9
Key: october     Value: 10
Key: november    Value: 11
Key: december    Value: 12

F:\Dart>
```

15.5 Update value for a key

The corresponding value of an existing key can be updated by assigning a new value. For example, consider the following KV pair:

Map<int, String> m1 = HashMap();
m1[1] = "aaa";

You can assign a new value for the key 1 as follows:

m1[1] = "bbb";

The key 1 will now hold "bbb".

Alternatively, you can use the update method as follows:

<map variable>.update([key], (value) => [new value]);
Example:
m1.update(1, (value) => "ccc");

Here is a program that shows the working of the update method:

```
//Map Demo -- Update
//HashMap is a part of daty:collection library
import 'dart:collection';
//Mandatory main function
void main() {
//Create a Map to store data of a person
Map<String, String> person = LinkedHashMap();
//Add entries
person['firstName'] = "Yulia";
person['lastName'] = "Alexander";
```

```
person['city'] = "Amsterdam";
person['country'] = "Netherlands";
//Print person map
print("\nperson map: $person\nSize: ${person.length}");
//Update value for city key
person['city'] = "Frankfurt";
//Update value for country key using the update method
person.update('country', (value) => 'Germany');
print("\n\nperson map (Updated): $person\nSize: ${person.length}");
}
```

Output:

15.6 Remove a key-value pair

A key-value pair can be removed from a map using the remove function as follows:

<map_variable>.remove(<key>);
Example:
m1.remove(1);

This function also returns the removed value. You can alternatively receive the returned value in a variable as follows:

<variable> = <map variable>.remove(<key>);

This method is particularly useful in a situation where the non-existent key has been specified. In such a case, null will be returned and the map will be subjected to no changes. Here is a Dart program that shows the working of this function:

//Map Demo -- Remove a KV pair

```
//Map class is a part of dart:core library
//HashMap is a part of daty:collection library
import 'dart:collection';
import 'dart:core';
//Mandatory main function
void main() {
//Create a Map to store data of a person
Map<String, String> person = LinkedHashMap();
//Add  entries
person['firstName'] = "Cynthia";
person['lastName'] = "Magsons";
person['city'] = "Calgary";
person['country'] = "Canada";
//Print person map
print("\nperson map: $person\nSize: ${person.length}");
//Remove city key
person.remove('city');
print("\n\nperson map (Updated): $person\nSize: ${person.length}");
}
```

Output:

15.7 Properties of the Map class

The Map class has several properties. Here is a brief look at the important ones:

isEmpty – returns true if the map is empty, returns false otherwise

isNotEmpty – returns false if the map is empty, returns true otherwise

length – returns the number of KV pairs present in the map

entries – returns all the entries (*Refer Section 15.4*) inside a map as an Iterable object

keys – returns all keys of as an Iterable object

values – returns all values as an Iterable object

Here is a program that shows the significance of these properties:

```
//Map Demo -- Useful map properties
//HashMap is a part of daty:collection library
import 'dart:collection';
//Mandatory main function
void main() {
//Declare a HashMap called days to store days of the week
//Key will be the name of the day (String) ans Sr. No. (int), and will be the value
Map<String, int> days = LinkedHashMap();
//Add entries
//Use [] operator
days['sunday'] = 1;
days['monday'] = 2;
days['tuesday'] = 3;
days['wednesday'] = 4;
days['thursday'] = 5;
days['friday'] = 6;
days['saturday'] = 7;
//Print map  days
print("\ndays map: \n$days");
//Demonstrate map properties
print("\ndays.isEmpty:                    ${days.isEmpty}\ndays.isNotEmpty:
${days.isNotEmpty}\ndays.length:                    ${days.length}\ndays.entries:
${days.entries}\ndays.keys: ${days.keys}\ndays.values: ${days.values}");
}
```

Output:

```
F:\Dart>dart run map6.dart

days map:
{sunday: 1, monday: 2, tuesday: 3, wednesday: 4, thursday: 5, friday: 6, saturda
y: 7}

days.isEmpty: false
days.isNotEmpty: true
days.length: 7
days.entries: (MapEntry(sunday: 1), MapEntry(monday: 2), MapEntry(tuesday: 3), .
.., MapEntry(friday: 6), MapEntry(saturday: 7))
days.keys: (sunday, monday, tuesday, wednesday, thursday, friday, saturday)
days.values: (1, 2, 3, 4, 5, 6, 7)

F:\Dart>_
```

15.8 Maps and loops

We have seen how the forEach method works. Let us now manually iterate through a map using for..in loop. To do this, we will first fetch all the keys using the keys property and iterate through the keys using the for..in loop. During each iteration, we will fetch the corresponding value:

```dart
//Map Demo -- iterate using loop and keys
//HashMap is a part of daty:collection library
import 'dart:collection';
//Mandatory main function
void main() {
//Declare a HashMap called days to store days of the week
//Key will be Sr. No. (int), and the name of the day will be the value (String)
Map<int, String> days = HashMap();
//Add entries
//Use [] operator
days[1] = "Sunday";
days[2] = "Monday";
days[3] = "Tuesday";
days[4] = "Wednesday";
days[5] = "Thursday";
days[6] = "Friday";
days[7] = "Saturday";
//Retrieve keys
var keys = days.keys;
//Iterate through keys using for in loop
for (var key in keys) {
print("\nKey: $key \t Value: ${days[key]}");
```

114

```
}
}
```

Output:

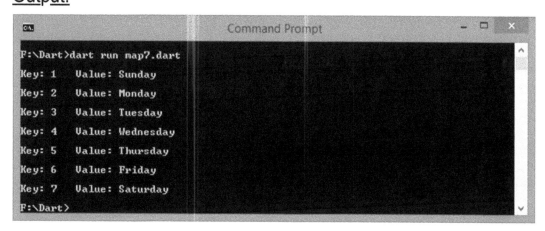

15.9 List of Maps

We have learnt important concepts regarding maps up to the previous section. This section is more of a programming challenge. Let us create a map to store personal details of a person. One map variable will store details of one person. We will then create a list of maps to store details of multiple people:

```
//Map Demo -- List of maps
//HashMap is a part of daty:collection library
import 'dart:collection';
//Mandatory main function

void main() {
//Create a list to store maps
var person_list = <Map> [];
//Create a Map to store data of a person
Map<String, String> person1 = LinkedHashMap();
//Add entries
person1['firstName'] = "Rahul";
person1['lastName'] = "Solanki";
person1['city'] = "Mumbai";
person1['country'] = "India";
//Create second person's map
Map<String, String> person2 = LinkedHashMap();
//Add entries
```

```
person2['firstName'] = "Krishna";
person2['lastName'] = "Sapkota";
person2['city'] = "Kathmandu";
person2['country'] = "Nepal";
//Create third person's map
Map<String, String> person3 = LinkedHashMap();
//Add  entries
person3['firstName'] = "Yaris";
person3['lastName'] = "Hossain";
person3['city'] = "Dhaka";
person3['country'] = "Bangladesh";
//Add all these to the list
person_list.add(person1);
person_list.add(person2);
person_list.add(person3);
//Iterate through list
var count = 0;
while (count < person_list.length) {
print("\nperson_list index: $count\n");
//Print detals of each map
person_list[count].forEach((key, value) {
print("Key: $key \t Value: $value");
});
//Increment count
count++;
}
}
```

Output:

```
F:\Dart>dart run map8.dart

person_list index: 0

Key: firstName    Value: Rahul
Key: lastName     Value: Solanki
Key: city         Value: Mumbai
Key: country      Value: India

person_list index: 1

Key: firstName    Value: Krishna
Key: lastName     Value: Sapkota
Key: city         Value: Kathmandu
Key: country      Value: Nepal

person_list index: 2

Key: firstName    Value: Yaris
Key: lastName     Value: Hossain
Key: city         Value: Dhaka
Key: country      Value: Bangladesh

F:\Dart>_
```

16. String

A string is a sequence of characters. We learnt the basics of strings in the first half of this book and have also used a lot of strings in different programs. Let us revise a few string concepts and also learn some more things.

16.1 String creation

A string can be created by enclosing characters either in single quotes or double quotes (either one, not mixed). If you want to include a single quote as a part of the string, the main string should be enclosed in double quotes and vice-versa. Other than this, any restricted character can be included inside a string by using the escape character backslash (\). Here is a general syntax of declaring a string:

var <String variable> = "<character sequence>";
OR
String <String variable> = "<character sequence">;

Multiline strings can be declared by enclosing the character sequence inside triple quotes (either single quotes or double quotes but not mixed). Here are a couple of examples:

var s1 = """We have come
towards the end
of this
book""";
String s2 = '''This has
been a
great
journey!''';

Let us write a program to demonstrate show how different types of strings work:

//String Demo -- String creation

```
//Mandatory main function
void main() {
//Create a few strings
//String in double quotes
var s1 = "This is the Strings chapter.";
//String in single quotes
String s2 = 'You have come this far!';
//Include quotes inside strings

var s3 = "To include a 'single quote' inside a string, the main string should be enclosed in double quotes.";
String s4 = "To include a 'double quote' inside a string, the main string should be enclosed in single quotes.";
//Escape characters
String s5 = "You can alternatively include any restricted characters inside a string by using the escape character \\ \nExample: Single quote - \' Double quote -\"";
//Multi line strings
var s6 = """This is
a multiline string""";
var s7 = '''This
is
another
multiline
string''';
///Print all strings
print("\ns1: $s1");
print("\ns2: $s2");
print("\ns3: $s3");
print("\ns4: $s4");
print("\ns5: $s5");
print("\ns6: $s6");
print("\ns7: $s7");
}
```

Output:

```
F:\Dart>dart run string1.dart
s1: This is the Strings chapter.
s2: You have come this far!
s3: To include a 'single quote' inside a string, the main string should be enclo
sed in double quotes.
s4: To include a 'double quote' inside a string, the main string should be enclo
sed in single quotes.
s5: You can alternatively include any restricted characters inside a string by u
sing the escape character \
Example: Single quote - ' Double quote -"
s6: This is
  a multiline string
s7: This
  is
  another
  multiline
  string
F:\Dart>
```

16.2 Concatenation

A string can be concatenated using the **+ operator** as follows:

<string variable> = <string 1> + ... + <string n>;
Example:
var s = s1 + " " + s2;

If string literals are to be concatenated, there is no need to use the + operators, the literals can be placed adjacent to one another as follows:

<string variable> = "<string literal 1>" "<string literal 2>" ... "<string literal n>";
Example:
var s = "This" " " "becomes a " "string!";

A non-string item can be added to a string by first converting it to a string using the **toString** function. Here is an example:

int x = 23;
double y = 76.12;
var s = "x is " + x.toString() + " y is " + y.toString();

A string can be repeated a number of times using the ***operator**.
Syntax:

> *<string variable> = <string> * <number of times to be repeated>*
> *//s will hold "HelloHelloHelloHelloHello"*
> *var s = "Hello" * 5;*

Here is a program that demonstrates all these concepts:

```
//String Demo -- String Concatenation
//Mandatory main function
void main() {
//Create a few strings
String capital1 = "Kigali";
String country1 = "Rwanda";
String capital2 = "Tunis";
String country2 = "Tunisia";
//Concatenate strings
var s1 = capital1 + " is the capital of " + country1;
var s2 = "Nairobi" " is the capital of " "Kenya";
var s3 = capital2 + " is the capital of " + country2;
//Create double variables
double pop_country1 = 11.8;
double pop_country2 = 12.6;
//Use toString to concatenate non string values
var s4 = "The population of " + country1 + "is approximately " + pop_country1.toString() + "
million";
var s5 = "The population of " + country2 + "is approximately " + pop_country2.toString() + "
million";
//Multiple capital2 5 times
var s6 = capital2 * 5;
//Print all strings
print("\ns1: $s1");
print("\ns2: $s2");
print("\ns3: $s3");
print("\ns4: $s4");
print("\ns5: $s5");
print("\ns6: $s6");
}
```

Output:

```
F:\Dart>dart run string2.dart
s1: Kigali is the capital of Rwanda
s2: Nairobi is the capital of Kenya
s3: Tunis is the capital of Tunisia
s4: The population of Rwandais approximately 11.8 million
s5: The population of Tunisiais approximately 12.6 million
s6: TunisTunisTunisTunisTunis
F:\Dart>
```

16.3 Properties of the String class

The String class has several properties. Here is a look at the important ones:

isEmpty – returns true if the string is empty, returns false otherwise

isNotEmpty – returns false if the string is empty, returns true otherwise

length – returns length of the string

Here is a program that shows the significance of these properties:

```
//String Demo -- String properties
//Mandatory main function
void main() {
//Create a few strings
var s1 = "Just a simple string.";
//Empty string
var s2 = "";
//Print string properties
print("\ns1: $s1");
print("\ns2: $s2");
print("\ns1 isEmpty: ${s1.isEmpty}");
print("\ns2 isEmpty: ${s2.isEmpty}");
print("\ns1 isNotEmpty: ${s1.isNotEmpty}");
print("\ns2 isNotEmpty: ${s2.isNotEmpty}");
print("\ns1  length: ${s1.length}");
print("\ns2 length: ${s2.length}");
}
```

Output:

```
F:\Dart>dart run string3.dart
s1: Just a simple string.
s2:
s1 isEmpty: false
s2 isEmpty: true
s1 isNotEmpty: true
s2 isNotEmpty: false
s1 length: 21
s2 length: 0
F:\Dart>
```

16.4 Strings and Loops

Individual characters of a string can be accessed using the index specified inside the **[ ] operator**. A string index starts at 0 and ends at one less than the size of the string (similar to lists). This makes it possible to iterate through the string using loops. Here is a programming example:

```dart
//String Demo -- String iteration
//Mandatory main function
void main() {
//Create a few strings
var s1 = "Dart!";
var s2 = "Sure it is!";
//Print strings
print("\ns1: $s1\nlength = ${s1.length}");
print("\ns2: $s2\nlength = ${s2.length}");
//Iterate using while loop
print("\ns1 printed character by character using while loop");
var i = 0;
while (i < s1.length) {
print("Character at $i: ${s1[i]}");
i++;
}
//Iterate using for loop
print("\ns2 printed character by character using for loop");
```

123

```
for (int j = 0; j < s2.length ; j++) {
print("Character at $j: ${s2[j]}");
}
}
```

Output:

```
F:\Dart>dart run string4.dart

s1: Dart!
length = 5

s2: Sure it is!
length = 11

s1 printed character by character using while loop
Character at 0: D
Character at 1: a
Character at 2: r
Character at 3: t
Character at 4: !

s2 printed character by character using for loop
Character at 0: S
Character at 1: u
Character at 2: r
Character at 3: e
Character at 4:
Character at 5: i
Character at 6: t
Character at 7:
Character at 8: i
Character at 9: s
Character at 10: !

F:\Dart>
```

Now that we know how to access individual characters of a string, let us write a function to accept a string as a parameter and return the reversed string:

```
//String Demo -- String creation
//String reversal function
String revString(String s) {
String rev = "";
var i = s.length - 1;
while (i >= 0) {
rev = rev + s[i];
i--;
}
return rev;
```

```
}
//Mandatory main function
void main() {
//Create a few strings
var s1 = "String reversal demo!";
//Call revString
var s2 = revString(s1);
//Print s1 s2
print("\nOriginal string: $s1\nReversed string: $s2");
}
```

Output:

```
F:\Dart>dart run string5.dart

Original string: String reversal demo!
Reversed string: !omed lasrever gnirtS

F:\Dart>
```

16.5 String comparison

The simplest way to compare two strings is using the *(==)* and *(!=)* operators. The (==) operator will return true if both the strings are exactly the same and false otherwise. Whereas, the (!=) will return true if both the string are not exactly the same and false otherwise. Here are a few examples:

var s1 = "book";
var s2 = "book";
var s3 = "book";
//false, case is different
var c1 = (s1 == s2);
//true
var c2 = (s2!= s3);
//true
var c3 = (s1 == s3);

There is another way to compare strings is using the **compareTo** function which checks their order. Here is the general syntax:

125

<variable> = <first string>.compareTo(<second string>);
Example:
var s1 = "WhatsApp";
var s2 = "Line";
var x = s1.compareTo(s2)

The compareTo function returns a positive value if the first string is ordered after the second string, returns a negative value if the first string is ordered before the second string and returns 0 if both strings are exactly the same. Here is a Dart program that demonstrates string comparison:

```
//String Demo -- String compare
//Mandatory main function
void main() {
//Create a few strings
var s1 = "Python";
var s2 = "Java";
var s3 = "Rust";
var s4 = "Python";
///Print all strings
print("\ns1: $s1");
print("\ns2: $s2");
print("\ns3: $s3");
print("\ns4: $s4");
//Perform string comparisons
var s1s2 = s1.compareTo(s2);
var s2s1 = s2.compareTo(s1);
var s3s4 = (s3 == s4);
var s3s2 = (s3 != s2);
var s1s4 = (s1 == s4);
var s2s4 = s2.compareTo(s4);
var s4s1 = s4.compareTo(s1);
//Print comparison results
print("\ns1.compareTo(s2): $s1s2");
print("\ns2.compareTo(s2): $s2s1");
print("\ns3 == s4: $s3s4");
print("\ns3 != s2: $s3s2");
print("\ns1 == s4: $s1s4");
print("\ns2.compareTo(s4): $s2s4");
print("\ns4.compareTo(s1): $s4s1");
}
```

Output:

```
F:\Dart>dart run string6.dart
s1: Python
s2: Java
s3: Rust
s4: Python
s1.compareTo(s2): 1
s2.compareTo(s2): -1
s3 == s4: false
s3 != s2: true
s1 == s4: true
s2.compareTo(s4): -1
s4.compareTo(s1): 0
F:\Dart>_
```

Now that we know how to access individual characters of a string and also to compare two different string, let us write a program to check if a string is a palindrome. If a string is the same as its reverse, then it is said to be a palindrome. For example, the word "malayalam" (*Trivia*: Malayalam is a regional Indian language native to the state of Kerala) will remain the same when it is reversed and thus is a palindrome. Here is the program:

```
//String Demo -- String palindrome
//String reversal function
String revString(String s) {
String rev = "";
var i = s.length - 1;
while (i >= 0) {
rev = rev + s[i];
i--;
}
return rev;
}
//Function to check if a given strig is a palindrome
void checkPalindrome (String s) {
var s_rev = revString(s);
```

127

```dart
if (s == s_rev) {
print("\n$s is a palindrome.");
} else {
print("\n$s is NOT a palindrome.");
}
}
//Mandatory main function
void main() {
//Create a few strings
var s1 = "book";
//Call  revString
var s2 = "madam";
//Print s1 s2
print("\ns1: $s1");
print("\ns2: $s2");
//Call checkPalindrome
checkPalindrome(s1);

checkPalindrome(s2);
}
```

Output:

```
F:\Dart>dart run string7.dart
s1: ebook
s2: madam
ebook is NOT a palindrome.
madam is a palindrome.
F:\Dart>_
```

16.6 Substring

A substring can be extracted from the main string using the substring function. Here is the general syntax:

<variable> = <string>.substring(<start index>, <end index (optional)>);

Example:

128

var s1 = "Hello from Dart!";
//Hello
var s2 = s1.substring(0, 4);
//Dart
var s3 = s1.substring(11);

Note: If the end index is not specified, it will be assumed as the end of the string.

Let us write a program to show this function in action:

```
//String Demo -- Substring
//Mandatory main function
void main() {
//Create a few strings
String s1 = "The month of June marks the beginning of the summer season in the northern hemisphere.";
String s2 = "Where as, the same month marks the beginning of the winter season in the southern hemisphere.";
//Print all strings
print("\ns1: $s1");
print("\ns2: $s2");
//Extract substrings
//Substring from index till the end
var s3 = s1.substring(13);
var s4 = s2.substring(31, 65);
print("\ns3: $s3");
print("\ns4: $s4");
}
```

Output:

```
F:\Dart>dart run string8.dart

s1: The month of June marks the beginning of the summer season in the northern h
emisphere.

s2: Where as, the same month marks the beginning of the winter season in the sou
thern hemisphere.

s3: June marks the beginning of the summer season in the northern hemisphere.

s4: the beginning of the winter season

F:\Dart>
```

16.7 Search inside a string

A matching pattern can be searched for inside a string using the following functions – **contains**, **indexOf** and **lastIndexOf**. The contains function returns true if the given pattern is present in the string and false otherwise. Whereas, the indexOf and lastIndexOf functions return the exact location of the matching pattern if found and -1 if not found. Here is the syntax:

<variable> = <string>.contains(<pattern>);
<variable> = <string>.indexOf(<pattern>, <optional start index>);
<variable> = <string>.lastIndexOf(<pattern>, <optional start index from the end>);

Let us understand the working of these functions with the help of a programming example:

```
//String Demo -- String search
//Mandatory main function
void main() {
//Create a few strings
String s1 = "December marks the beginning of the winter season in the northern hemisphere.";
String s2 = "December marks the beginning of the summer season in the southern hemisphere.";
//Print all strings
print("\ns1: $s1");
print("\ns2: $s2");
//Search operation results
print("\ns1.contains('summer'): ${s1.contains('summer')}");
print("\ns1.contains('winter'): ${s1.contains('winter')}");
print("\ns2.contains('summer'): ${s2.contains('summer')}");
print("\ns2.contains('winter'): ${s2.contains('winter')}");
print("\ns1.indexOf('the'): ${s1.indexOf('the')}");
print("\ns1.indexOf('the', 16): ${s1.indexOf('the', 16)}");
print("\ns1.lastIndexOf('the'): ${s1.lastIndexOf('the')}");
print("\ns1.lastIndexOf('the', 19): ${s1.lastIndexOf('the', 19)}");
print("\ns1.contains('spring'): ${s1.contains('spring')}");
print("\ns2.contains('fall'): ${s1.contains('fall')}");
print("\ns2.indexOf('March'): ${s1.indexOf('March')}");
}
```

Output:

```
Command Prompt                                    -  □  ×

F:\Dart>dart run string9.dart
s1: December marks the beginning of the winter season in the northern hemisphere
.
s2: December marks the beginning of the summer season in the southern hemisphere
.
s1.contains('summer'): false
s1.contains('winter'): true
s2.contains('summer'): true
s2.contains('winter'): false
s1.indexOf('the'): 15
s1.indexOf('the', 16): 32
s1.lastIndexOf('the'): 60
s1.lastIndexOf('the', 19): 15
s1.contains('spring'): false
s2.contains('fall'): false
s2.indexOf('March'): -1
F:\Dart>
```

16.8 Useful String class methods

Here are some of the useful methods of the String class:

toUpperCase – converts all alphabets to upper case

toLowerCase – converts all alphabets to lower case

trimLeft – removes all white spaces at the beginning of the string

trimRight – removes all white spaces at the end of the string

trim – removes all white spaces at both beginning and at the end of the string

split – splits a string into a list of strings, separated by a delimiter

Here is a programming example that demonstrates the usage of these functions:

```
void main() {
//Create a few strings
String s1 = "Spain lies in the European continent";
```

```
String s2 = " \tJapan lies in the Asian continent ";
print("\ns1: $s1");
print("\ns2: $s2");
//Upper and lower  case
print("\ns1.toUpperCase(): " + s1.toUpperCase());
print("\ns1.toLowerCase(): " + s1.toLowerCase());
//Trim functions
print("\ns2.trimLeft(): " + s2.trimLeft());
print("\ns2.trimLRight(): " + s2.trimRight());
print("\ns2.trim(): " + s2.trim());
print("\ns1.split(' '):\n${s1.split(' ')}");
}
```

Output:

17. Introduction to Object Oriented Programming

Object Oriented Programming (abbreviated as *OOP*) is a programming paradigm where the emphasis is made on data over procedure. OOP in Dart is such a vast topic that a separate book can be written just to teach these concepts and a lot of OOP techniques are quiet advanced in nature suitable only for seasoned developers.

In this section, we will only learn about the basics of OOP, enough for you to get acquainted with this important paradigm. The fundamentals of OOP lie in a couple of basic concepts – *Classes* and *Objects*. A Class is a user defined data type with *data members* (variables) and *member functions* (class methods) which can access data members. An Object is an instance of a class having its own data members as defined in the class.

Let us understand this concept with a simple example. Consider you want to store personal details of people. Details could be things like name, address, age, etc. To do this, you can define a class called *Person* where *name, address, age,* etc. could be defined as variables inside the class. These variables become data members or *properties* of class. When details of a person need to be stored, an object of this class need to be created (also known as an instance). Each object will have its own copy of name, address, age, etc. and hence can store details of an individual person.

17.1 Introduction to Classes and Objects

A class can be defined using the *Class* keyword as follows:

```
class <Class Name> {
//Data members
...
...
```

...
//Member functions
...
...
...
}
Example:
class Person {
String name = "";
String address = "";
int age = -1;
}

Note:

- Data members should be given an initial value.
- It is ideal to define a class outside all functions so that it can be accessed from anywhere.

Objects of a class can be created using the following syntax:

<Class Name> <Object Name> = <Class Name>();
Example:
Person p1 = Person();
Person p2 = Person();
//p1 and p2 are now two different objects of type person.
//Both p1 and p2 now have their own copies of name, address and age

Note: Person() is actually a constructor. More details on this are covered in **Section 17.3**.

Data members of a class can be accessed using the **dot (.) operator:**

p1.name = "Yuri";
p1.address = "Tashkent";

p1.age = 43;
p2.name = "Willow";
p2.address = "Cape Town";
p2.age = 32;

To check the type of an object, you can use the ***runtimeType*** property Eg. ***p1.runtimeType***.

Let us write a Dart program to create a class called ***Smartphone*** in which we will have data members to store the specifications of smartphones such as make, model, ram, etc. Here is the program:

```dart
//Object Oriented Programming
//Introduction to classed and objects
//Set data members
//Smartphone class definition
class Smartphone {
//Define data members and initialize
String make = "";
String model = "";
String chipset = "";
int ram = 0;
int storage = 0;
double screen_size = 0.0;
}
//Mandatory main function
void main() {
//Create objects of Smartphone type
//Object s1
Smartphone s1 = Smartphone();
//Set data members for s1
s1.make = "Google";
s1.model = "Pixel 6";
s1.chipset = "Google Tensor";
s1.ram = 8;
s1.storage = 256;
s1.screen_size = 6.4;
//Object s2
Smartphone s2 = Smartphone();
//Set data members for s2
s2.make = "Samsung";
s2.model = "Galaxy S22";
s2.chipset = "Exynos 220";
```

```
s2.ram = 8;
s2.storage = 128;
s2.screen_size = 6.1;
//Print data members of s1 and s2
print("\nObject s1 (type: ${s1.runtimeType}):");
print("\nmake: ${s1.make}");
print("model: ${s1.model}");
print("chipset: ${s1.chipset}");
print("ram: ${s1.ram}");
print("storage: ${s1.storage}");
print("screen_size: ${s1.screen_size}");
print("\nObject s2 (type: ${s2.runtimeType}):");
print("\nmake: ${s2.make}");
print("model: ${s2.model}");
print("chipset: ${s2.chipset}");
print("ram: ${s2.ram}");
print("storage: ${s2.storage}");
print("screen_size: ${s2.screen_size}");
}
```

Output:

17.2 Member functions

Although it is possible to access data members of a class using the dot operator, the ideal way to do it is to define functions inside

136

the class and access the data members from there. Here is an example:

```
class Person {
String name = "";
String address = "";
int age = -1;
//member functions
void getDetails(String n, String add, int a) {
name = n;
address = add;
age = a;
}
}
```

Once the object is created, member function for that particular object can be invoked using the dot operator. Syntax:

```
Person p1 = Person();
p1.getDetails("Bob", "Erfurt", 38);
```

We will modify the previous programming example to access data members of Smartphone class using member functions:

```
//Object Oriented Programming
//Introduction to classed and objects
//Use member functions
//Smartphone class definition
class Smartphone {
//Define data members and initialize
String make = "";
String model = "";
String chipset = "";
int ram = 0;
int storage = 0;
double screen_size = 0.0;
//Define member functions
//Function to set parameters of the objects
void setData(String Make, String Model, String Chipset, int Ram, int Storage, double Screen_size) {
//Assign function parameters to Class's data members
```

```dart
        make = Make;
        model = Model;
        chipset = Chipset;
        ram = Ram;
        storage = Storage;
        screen_size = Screen_size;
    }
    //Function to print data
    void showData() {
        print("\nObject type: ${runtimeType}:");
        print("\nmake: ${make}");
        print("model: ${model}");
        print("chipset: ${chipset}");
        print("ram: ${ram}");
        print("storage: ${storage}");
        print("screen_size: ${screen_size}");
    }
}
//Mandatory main function
void main() {
    //Create objects of Smartphone type
    //Object s1
    Smartphone s1 = Smartphone();
    //Invode setData to set data members of s1
    s1.setData("Asus", "ROG Phone 5s Pro", "Snapdragon 888+ 5G", 18, 512, 6.78);
    //Object s2
    Smartphone s2 = Smartphone();
    //Invode setData to set data members of s2
    s2.setData("Nokia", "C21 Plus", "Unisoc SC9863A", 4, 64, 6.52);
    //Print data of both objects
    s1.showData();
    s2.showData();
}
```

Output:

```
Command Prompt                                    _ □ ✕

F:\Dart>dart run oop2.dart

Object type: Smartphone:

make: Asus
model: ROG Phone 5s Pro
chipset: Snapdragon 888+ 5G
ram: 18
storage: 512
screen_size: 6.78

Object type: Smartphone:

make: Nokia
model: C21 Plus
chipset: Unisoc SC9863A
ram: 4
storage: 64
screen_size: 6.52

F:\Dart>
```

Note: If you notice – data members of the class and function parameters of setData function, different cases are used to avoid ambiguity (for example – make and Make, chipset and Chipset, etc.). There is an even better way to avoid ambiguity – using *this* keyword. You can have the exact same names for data members and function parameters. However, when you access data members, you can use *this.<data member>*.

17.3 Constructors

A constructor is a special kind of a member function which has the same name as that of the class. A constructor gets invoked automatically when an object is created. If you recall the code snippet from *Section 17.1*, *Person()* constructor has the same name as class *Person*. Constructors are used to initialize objects. It is possible (and also recommended) to define your own constructor for a class. If no constructor is defined, a default constructor gets invoked (implicit). Here is an example:

class Person {
String name = "";
String address = "";
int age = -1;

139

```
//Constructor
Person(String n, String add, int a) {
name = n;
address = add;
age = a;
}
```

Let us write a Dart program to include a constructor in the previous programming example:

```
//Object Oriented Programming
//Introduction to classed and objects
//Constructors
//Smartphone class definition
class Smartphone {
//Define data members and initialize
String make = "";
String model = "";
String chipset = "";
int ram = 0;
int storage = 0;
double screen_size = 0.0;
//Constructor to initialize objects
Smartphone(String make, String model, String chipset, int ram, int storage, double
screen_size) {
//Assign parameters to Class's data members
this.make = make;
this.model = model;
this.chipset = chipset;
this.ram = ram;
this.storage = storage;
this.screen_size = screen_size;
}
//Function to print data
void showData() {
print("\nObject type: ${this.runtimeType}:");
print("\nmake: ${this.make}");
print("model: ${this.model}");
print("chipset: ${this.chipset}");
print("ram: ${this.ram}");
print("storage: ${this.storage}");
print("screen_size: ${this.screen_size}");
}
```

```
}
//Mandatory main function
void main() {
//Create objects of Smartphone type
//Object s1
//Call the parameterized constructor, pass initial values for s1
Smartphone s1 = Smartphone("Apple", "iPhone 13", "Apple A15 Bionic", 4, 128, 6.1);
//Object s2
//Call the parameterized constructor, pass initial values for s2
Smartphone s2 = Smartphone("Xperia", "1 III", "Snapdragon 888 5G", 12, 256, 6.5);
//Invode setData to set data members of s2
//Print data of both objects
s1.showData();
s2.showData();
}
```

Output:

18. Final Words

Dart has a lot of scope for developing web applications, web services, server side applications and mobile applications. In this book, I have focused on concepts keeping the absolute beginner in mind. The founding concepts have been given more attention and have been covered in depth. If you liked this language and understood the concepts explained in this book well, there is no reason why you should stop learning! There are plenty of resources on the internet. I recommend Dart's official language reference page – https://dart.dev/guides/language (As time goes by, links may change. A simple search on your favourite search engine should get you to the correct page).

For those who want to learn advanced Dart concepts, I recommend learning concepts such as exception handling, advanced OOP concepts such as inheritance, IO, Dart for Web is always an option for those who want to learn web development. If you are remotely interested in mobile application development, I suggest learning ***Flutter framework***. It is the next big thing and it is here to stay. Dart being its programming language makes an even stronger case for learning it.

Hope you have learnt something of value from my book.

Good luck!

www.ingramcontent.com/pod-product-compliance
Lightning Source LLC
Chambersburg PA
CBHW080534060326
40690CB00022B/5128